Florida
Real Estate Practice Exams
for 2015-2016

by

Jim Bainbridge, J.D.

© 2015

City Breeze Publishing LLC
P.O. Box 12650
Marina del Rey, California 90250

ISBN: 978-1-939526-29-8

PRINTED IN THE UNITED STATES OF AMERICA

About the Author

Jim Bainbridge is a graduate of Harvard Law School and has been an active member of the California Bar for more than 30 years. He is a licensed California real estate broker, and a past recipient of a National Science Foundation Fellowship for graduate studies in mathematics at UC Berkeley. He is the author of *Pearson VUE Real Estate Exam Prep 2015-2016*, *California Real Estate Principles and License Preparation*, and numerous works that have been published in more than 50 journals in the USA, UK, Canada, Australia, Japan, and the Netherlands.

Mr. Bainbridge is also a member of the Real Estate Educators Association (REEA) and has been recognized as a Certified Distance Education Instructor by IDECC, which is a function of the Association of Real Estate License Law Officials.

DISCLAIMER and LIMIT of LIABILITY

Introduction

Thank you for purchasing *Florida Real Estate Practice Exams for 2015-2016*. This book is intended to help you prepare for — and pass — the Florida Real Estate Exam. This book consists of:

- four 100-multiple-choice-question Florida real estate practice exams;

- detailed answers given for all of the questions, allowing you to assess your strengths and weaknesses — and to hone your test-taking skills — before exam day;

- a comprehensive review of the real estate math that you are expected to know for the Florida exam;

- a useful glossary of over 600 key real estate terms for test preparation and reference, and;

- tips on preparing for and taking the Florida exam.

Of course, this book of practice exams is no substitute for a study of the real estate principles contained in pre-licensing courses. Before you take these practice exams, you should have a thorough knowledge of these real estate principles. If you do not, you may become discouraged by your scores on these practice exams — and confidence will serve you well on your quest to pass the Florida exam and become a real estate licensee.

Table of Contents

EXAM TEST-TAKING TIPS..6

DEFINITIONS OF KEY REAL ESTATE TERMS...8

REAL ESTATE MATH 41

Section 1: Basic Math Concepts 41

Section 2: Calculations for Transactions, Including Mortgage Calculations....................................... 44

Section 3: Property Tax Calculations 44

Section 4: Prorations (utilities, rent, property taxes, insurance, etc.).. 45

Section 5: Calculations for Valuation... 50

PRACTICE EXAM #1: 53

ANSWERS TO PRACTICE EXAM #1:..74

PRACTICE EXAM #2: 82

ANSWERS TO PRACTICE EXAM #2:..102

PRACTICE EXAM #3: 109

ANSWERS TO PRACTICE EXAM #3:..129

PRACTICE EXAM #4: 136

ANSWERS TO PRACTICE EXAM #4:..157

EXAM TEST-TAKING TIPS

- The Florida real estate exam potentially covers a vast amount of real estate knowledge; therefore, taking practice exams — and studying the answers that you get wrong — during the weeks immediately prior to exam day can be highly beneficial.

- You will be graded on the number of correct answers you give. You will not be penalized for giving incorrect answers. Therefore, it is important to answer all of the questions, even if you are not sure of the correct answer. Often, of the four possible answers presented, at least two answers are clearly wrong. Of the remaining two, both might appear correct, in which case you should choose the answer that you feel is the better one. If you cannot decide which one is the better, take your best guess — you'll probably have about a 50-50 chance of being correct.

- Take the time to read each question carefully. It is altogether too easy to interpret a question in a way that you expect the question to read, rather than as it is actually stated. This is especially true for questions that are stated in the negative ("it is not true that…" or "which of the following is false"). Other keywords that can significantly alter the meaning of a question are "except," "but," "if," and "generally."

- Do not rush to choose an answer just because you are relatively certain that it is true. This is because there may be two or more answers given that correctly answer the question, in which case such answers as "both a and b" or "all of the above" may be the best, and correct, answer.

- If math is your most problematic and anxiety producing area, consider saving the math questions to the end and coming back to them when you have completed the rest of the exam. This will prevent you from becoming frustrated and discouraged through most of the exam and will likely give you more time to figure out the correct answers to the math questions.

- You should try to estimate the correct answer to math questions before you begin your calculations. If you find that your estimate is far different from the result of your calculation, carefully go back and check your calculation. Also, be aware that the possible answers presented for math questions usually contain answers that examinees can arrive at by making some common error, such as by calculating based on the number of years rather than on the number of months. Therefore, just because the result of your calculation exactly matches one of the possible answers does not mean that your result is correct.

- Additionally, math real estate questions often use "none of the above" as the fourth possible answer. This means that if you do not get an answer that matches one of the first three possible answers, either your calculation was incorrect or the correct exam answer is "none of the above."

- Because the extensive glossary included in this book includes terms often found on Florida real estate exams, it is recommended that you review these important key real estate terms at least once each week prior to taking the official Florida exam.

- Finally, if you complete the exam early, as many examinees do, take the remaining time to read over as many of the questions as you can to be sure that you did not make the all-too-common mistake of misreading certain questions the first time around. As you take the following practice exam, you will probably find that you make several "foolish" errors — errors that result not from your lack of knowledge, but from your failure to carefully read certain questions that can at times appear to be a bit tricky. Don't let such "foolish" errors spoil the result of your official exam.

Good luck! And may you have a long and rewarding career as a real estate licensee.

DEFINITIONS OF KEY REAL ESTATE TERMS

1031 exchange — under Internal Revenue Code section 1031, a tax-deferred exchange of "like kind" properties.

1099-S Reporting — a report to be submitted on IRS Form 1099-S by escrow agents to report the sale of real estate, giving the seller's name, Social Security number, and the gross sale proceeds.

abandonment — failure to occupy or use property that may result in the extinguishment of a right or interest in the property.

abatement — a legal action to remove a nuisance.

abstract of judgment — a summary of the essential provisions of a court monetary judgment that can be recorded in the county recorder's office of the county or counties in which the judgment debtor owns property to create a judgment lien against such properties.

abstract of title — a chronological summary of all grants, liens, wills, judicial proceedings, and other records that affect the property's title.

abstractor — the person who prepares an abstract of title.

acceleration clause — a clause in either a promissory note, a security instrument, or both that states that upon default the lender has the option of declaring the entire balance of outstanding principal and interest due and payable immediately.

acceptance — consent (by an offeree) to an offer made (by an offeror) to enter into and be bound by a contract.

accession — the acquisition of additional property by the natural processes of accretion, reliction, or avulsion, or by the human processes of the addition of fixtures or improvements made in error.

accretion — a natural process by which the owner of riparian or littoral property acquires additional land by the gradual accumulation of soil through the action of water.

accrued depreciation — depreciation that has happened prior to the date of valuation.

acknowledgment — a written declaration signed by a person before a duly authorized officer, usually a notary public, acknowledging that the signing is voluntary.

active investor — an investor who actively contributes to the management of the business invested in.

ad valorem — a Latin phrase meaning "according to value." The term is usually used regarding property taxation.

adjustable-rate mortgage (ARM) — a mortgage under which interest rates applicable to the loan vary over the term of the loan.

adjusted cost basis — the dollar amount assigned to a property after additions of improvements and deductions for depreciation and losses are made to the property's acquisition cost.

adjustment period — the time intervals in an adjustable-rate mortgage during which interest rates are not adjusted.

administrator — a person appointed by a probate court to conduct the affairs and distribute the assets of a decedent's estate when there was no executor named in the will or there was no will.

advance fee — a fee charged in advance of services rendered.

adverse possession — the process by which unauthorized possession and use of another's property can ripen into ownership of that other's property without compensation.

after-acquired interests — all interests in a property acquired subsequent to a transfer of the property.

affirmative covenant — a contractual promise to do certain acts, such as to maintain a party wall, the remedy for breach thereof being either monetary damages or injunctive relief, not forfeiture.

age-life method — *see*, straight-line method.

agency — the representation of a principal by an agent.

agent — a person who represents another.

alienation clause — a due-on-sale clause

alluvium — addition to land acquired by the gradual accumulation of soil through the action of water.

ambulatory instrument — a document that can be changed or revoked, such as a will.

amended public report — a report that a subdivider must apply for if, after the issuance of a final public report, new conditions arise that affect the value of the subdivision parcels.

Americans with Disabilities Act — a federal act that prohibits discrimination against persons with disabilities, where "disability" is defined as "a physical or mental impairment that substantially limits a major life activity."

amortization — in general, the process of decreasing or recovering an amount over a period of time; as applied to real estate loans, the process of reducing the loan principal over the life of the loan.

anchor bolt — a bolt inserted into concrete that secures structural members to the foundation.

annual percentage rate (APR) — expresses the effective annual rate of the cost of borrowing, which includes all finance charges, such as interest, prepaid finance charges, prepaid interest, and service fees.

appraisal — an estimate of the value of property resulting from an analysis and evaluation made by an appraiser of facts and data regarding the property.

appreciation — an increase in value due to any cause.

appropriation, right of — the legal right to take possession of and use for beneficial purposes water from streams or other bodies of water.

appurtenance — an object, right or interest that is incidental to the land and goes with or pertains to the land.

asbestos — a naturally occurring mineral composite that once was used extensively as insulation in residential and commercial buildings, in brake pads, and in fire-retardant products, such as furniture.

As asbestos ages, it breaks down to small fibers that, if inhaled in sufficient quantity over sufficient time, can cause a variety of ailments, including a type of cancer known as mesothelioma.

assignment — the transfer of the rights and obligations of one party (the assignor) to a contract to another party (the assignee); a transfer of a tenant's entire interest in the tenant's leased premises.

assumption — an adoption of an obligation that primarily rests upon another person, such as when a purchaser agrees to be primarily liable on a loan taken out by the seller.

attachment lien — a prejudgment lien on property, obtained to ensure the availability of funds to pay a judgment if the plaintiff prevails.

attorney in fact — a holder of a power of attorney.

average price per square foot — the average price per square foot for a given set of properties is arrived at by adding the per-square-foot cost of each property in the set by the number of properties in the set.

avulsion — a process that occurs when a river or stream suddenly carries away a part of a bank and deposits it downstream, either on the same or opposite bank.

back-end ratio — the ratio of total monthly expenses, including housing expenses and long-term monthly debt payments, to monthly gross income.

balloon payment — a payment, usually the final payment, of an installment loan that is significantly greater than prior payments — "significantly greater" generally being considered as being more than twice the lowest installment payment paid over the loan term.

bankruptcy — a legal process conducted in a United States Bankruptcy court, in which a person declares his or her inability to pay debts.

beam — a horizontal member of a building attached to framing, rafters, etc., that transversely supports a load.

bearing wall — a wall that supports structures (such as the roof or upper floors) above it. In condominiums, non-bearing walls are owned by the individual condominium owners, whereas bearing walls usually are property owned in common.

beneficiary — (1) the lender under a deed of trust, (2) one entitled to receive property under a will, (3) one for whom a trust is created.

bequeath — to transfer personal property by a will.

bequest — a gift of personal property by will.

bilateral contract — a contract in which a promise given by one party is exchanged for a promise given by the other party.

bill of sale — a written document given by a seller to a purchaser of personal property.

blanket mortgage — a mortgage used to finance two or more parcels of real estate.

blight — as used in real estate, the decline of a property or neighborhood as a result of adverse land use, destructive economic forces, failure to maintain the quality of older structures, failure to maintain foreclosed homes, etc.

blind ad — an advertisement that does not disclose the identity of the agent submitting the advertisement for publication.

blockbusting — the illegal practice of representing that prices will decline, or crime increase, or other negative effects will occur because of the entrance of minorities into particular areas.

board foot — a unit of measure of the volume of lumber, equivalent to the volume of lumber of 1 square foot and 1 inch thick; 144 cubic inches.

bona fide — in good faith; authentic; sincere; without intent to deceive.

book depreciation — a mathematical calculation used by tax authorities and accountants to determine a depreciation deduction from gross income.

book sale — a "sale" for accounting purposes regarding tax-delinquent property; this "sale" does not entail an actual transfer property.

boot — cash or other not like-kind property received in an exchange.

bridge loan — a short-term loan (often referred to as a swing loan) that is used by a borrower until permanent financing becomes available.

broker — a person who, for a compensation or an expectation of compensation, represents another in the transfer of an interest in real property.

brownfields — as defined by the EPA, "real property, the expansion, redevelopment, or reuse of which may be complicated by the presence or potential presence of a hazardous substance, polluted, or contaminant."

BTU (British Thermal Unit) — A measure of heating (or cooling) capacity equivalent to the amount of heat required to raise the temperature of 1 pound of water 1° Fahrenheit (from 39°F to 40°F).

buffer zone — in zoning, a strip of land to separate, or to ease the transition from, one use to another, such as a park separating a residential zone from a commercial zone, or a commercial or industrial zone separating residential zones from busy streets or highways.

bulk sale — a sale, not in the ordinary course of the seller's business, of more than half of the value of the seller's inventory as of the date of the bulk sale agreement.

bundle of rights — rights the law attributes to ownership of property.

business opportunity — involves the sale or lease of the assets of an existing business enterprise or opportunity, including the goodwill of the business or opportunity, enabling the purchaser or lessee to begin a business.

buyer's agent — a real estate broker appointed by a buyer to find property for the buyer.

capital asset — permanent, non-inventory assets held for personal or investment purposes, such as householders' homes, household furnishings, stocks, bonds, land, buildings, and machinery.

capital gain — the amount by which the net sale proceeds from the sale of a capital asset exceeds the adjusted cost value of the asset.

capitalization approach — *see*, income approach

capitalization rate — the annual net income of a property divided by the initial investment in, or value of, the property; the rate that an appraiser estimates is the yield rate expected by investors from comparable properties in current market conditions.

carryover —under an adjustable-rate loan, an increase in the interest rate not imposed because of an interest-rate cap that is carried over to later rate adjustments.

caulking — a putty-like material used to seal cracks and joints to make tight against leakage of air or water, as in making windows watertight.

CC&Rs — an abbreviation of "covenants, conditions, and restrictions" — often used to refer to restrictions recorded by a developer on an entire subdivision.

certificate of occupancy — a written document issued by a local governmental agency, stating that a structure intended for occupancy has been completed, inspected, and found to be habitable.

chain of title — a complete chronological history of all of the documents affecting title to the property.

chattel real — personal property that contains some interest in real property, the most common example being a lease.

Civil Rights Act of 1866 — a federal law enacted during Reconstruction that stated that people of any race may enjoy the right to enforce contracts, to sue, be parties, and give evidence, to inherit, purchase, lease, sell, hold, and convey real and personal property, and to full and equal benefit of all laws.

Civil Rights Act of 1968 — a federal law (often referred to as the Fair Housing Act) that prohibited discrimination in housing based on race, creed, or national origin. An amendment to this Act in 1974 added prohibition against discrimination based on gender, and an amendment in 1988 added prohibition against discrimination based on a person's disabilities or familial status.

closing — in reference to an escrow, a process leading up to, and concluding with, a buyer's receiving the deed to the property and the seller's receiving the purchase money.

cloud on title — any document, claim, lien, or other encumbrance that may impair the title to real property or cast doubt on the validity of the title.

coastal zone — a region where significant interaction of land and sea processes occurs.

Coastal Zone Management Act (CZMA) — a federal act intended to protect coastal zones, including the fish and wildlife that inhabit those zones, of the Atlantic, Pacific, and Arctic oceans, the Gulf of Mexico, Long Island Sound, and the Great Lakes from harmful effects due to residential, commercial, and industrial development.

collar beam — a beam connecting pairs of opposite rafters well above the attic floor.

column — a circular or rectangular vertical structural member that supports the weight of the structure above it.

commercial acre — the buildable part of an acre that remains after subtracting land needed for streets, sidewalks, and curbs.

commingling — regarding trust fund accounts, the act of improperly segregating the funds belonging to the agent from the funds received and held on behalf of another; the mixing of separate and community property.

commission — an agent's compensation for performance of his or her duties as an agent; in real estate, it is usually a percent of the selling price of the property or, in the case of leases, of rentals.

common interest development (CID) — a subdivision in which purchasers own or lease a separate lot, unit, or interest, and have an undivided interest or membership in a portion of the common area of the subdivision.

community apartment project — a development in which an undivided interest in the land is coupled with the right of exclusive occupancy of an apartment located thereon.

community property — property owned jointly by a married couple or by registered domestic partners, as distinguished from separate property. As a general rule, property acquired by a spouse or registered domestic partner through his/her skills or personal efforts is community property.

comparable property — a property similar to the subject property being appraised that recently sold at arm's length, where neither the buyer nor the seller was acting under significant financial pressure.

comparative market analysis (CMA) — a comparison analysis made by real estate brokers using recent sales, and current listings, of similar nearby homes to determine the list price for a subject property.

competitive market analysis (CMA) — *see*, comparative market analysis.

compound interest — the type of interest that is generated when accumulated interest is reinvested to generate interest earnings from previous interest earnings.

concealment — the act of preventing disclosure of something.

condemnation proceeding — a judicial or administrative proceeding to exercise power of eminent domain.

condition subsequent — a condition written into the deed of a fee estate that, if violated, may "defeat" the estate and lead to its loss and reversion to the grantor.

conditional use — a zoning exception for special uses such as churches, schools, and hospitals that wish to locate to areas zoned exclusively for residential use.

condominium — a residential unit owned in severalty, the boundaries of which are usually walls, floors, and ceilings, and an undivided interest in portions of the real property, such as halls, elevators, and recreational facilities.

conduit — a (usually) metal pipe in which electrical wiring is installed.

conflict of interest — a situation in which an individual or organization is involved in several *potentially* competing interests, creating a risk that one interest *might* unduly influence another interest.

conforming loan — a loan in conformance with FHFA guidelines.

consideration — anything of value given or promised, such as money, property, services, or a forbearance, to induce another to enter into a contract.

conspiracy — in antitrust law, occurs when two or more persons agree to act and the agreed-upon action has the effect of restraining trade.

construction mortgage — a security instrument used to secure a short-term loan to finance improvements to a property.

constructive eviction — a breach by the landlord of the covenant of habitability or quiet enjoyment.

constructive notice — (1) notice provided by public records; (2) notice of information provided by law to a person who, by exercising reasonable diligence, could have discovered the information.

contingency — an event that may, but is not certain to, happen, the occurrence upon which the happening of another event is dependent.

contract — a contract is an agreement to do or to forbear from doing a certain thing.

conventional loan — a mortgage loan that is not FHA insured or VA guaranteed.

conversion — the unauthorized misappropriation and use of another's funds or other property.

cooperating broker — a broker who attempts to find a buyer for a property listed by another broker.

cost approach — an appraisal approach that obtains the market value of the subject property by adding the value of the land (unimproved) of the subject property to the depreciated value of the cost (if currently purchased new) of the improvements on subject property.

cost recovery — the recoupment of the purchase price of a property through book depreciation; the tax concept of depreciation.

cost-to-cure method — a method of calculating depreciation by estimating the cost of curing the curable depreciation and adding it to the value of the incurable depreciation.

counteroffer — a new offer by an offeree that acts as a rejection of an offer by an offeror.

coupled with an interest — an aspect of an agency that refers to the agent's having a financial interest in the subject of the agency, which has the legal effect of making the appointment of the agent irrevocable.

covenant — a contractual promise to do or not do certain acts, such as on a property, the remedy for breach thereof being either monetary damages or injunctive relief, not forfeiture.

crawlspace — the space between the ground and the first floor that permits access beneath the building.

credit bid — a bid at a foreclosure sale made by the beneficiary up to the amount owed to the beneficiary.

credits — in reference to an escrow account, items payable to a party. This definition of a debit does not conform to its use in double-entry bookkeeping or accounting.

cubic-foot method — a method of estimating the replacement or reproduction cost of a structure that is similar to the square-foot method except that it uses the volume of recently constructed similar buildings. This method often is used for warehouses and other industrial buildings

curable depreciation — depreciation that results from physical deterioration or functional obsolescence that can be repaired or replaced at a cost that is less than or equal to the value added to the property.

debits — in reference to an escrow account, items payable by a party. This definition of a debit does not conform to its use in double-entry bookkeeping or accounting.

deed — a document that when signed by the grantor and legally delivered to the grantee conveys title to real property.

deed in lieu of foreclosure — a method of avoiding foreclosure by conveying to a lender title to a property lieu of the lender's foreclosing on the property.

defeasance clause — a provision in a loan that states that when the loan debt has been fully paid, the lender must release the property from the lien so that legal title free from the lien will be owned by the borrower.

defendant — the one against whom a lawsuit is brought.

deferred maintenance — any type of depreciation that has not been corrected by diligent maintenance.

deficiency judgment — a judgment given to a lender in an amount equal to the balance of the loan minus the net proceeds the lender receives after a judicial foreclosure.

deliberate misrepresentation — *see*, intentional misrepresentation

designated sales associates — in Florida, sales associates designated by the sales associates' employing broker, at the request of the broker's customers, to act as single agents for different customers in the same transaction, where the transaction is not a residential sale and where the buyer and seller each have assets of $1 million or more.

demand — the level of desire for a product.

Depository Institutions Deregulation and Monetary Control Act (DIDMC) — a federal law that exempts from state usury laws interest paid on residential mortgage loans.

deposit receipt — a written document indicating that a good-faith deposit has been received as part of an offer to purchase real property; also called a purchase and sale agreement.

depreciation — the loss in value due to any cause.

depreciation deduction — an annual tax allowance for the depreciation of property.

devise — (1) (noun) a gift of real property by will; (2) (verb) to transfer real property by a will.

devisee — a recipient of real property through a will.

discounted rate — a rate (also called a teaser rate) on an adjustable-rate mortgage that is less than the fully indexed rate.

discount points — a form of prepaid interest on a mortgage, or a fee paid to a lender to cover cost the making of a loan. The fee for one discount point is equal to 1% of the loan amount.

disintegration — the phase when a property's usefulness is in decline and constant upkeep is necessary.

divided agency — an agency in which the agent represents both the seller and the buyer without obtaining the consent of both.

dominant tenement — land that is benefited by an easement appurtenant.

dormer — a projecting structure built out from a sloping roof that is used to provide windows and additional headroom for the upper floor.

down payment — the amount of money that a lender requires a purchaser to pay toward the purchase price.

drywall — prefabricated sheets or panels nailed to studs to form an interior wall or partition.

dual agent — a real estate broker who, in a fiduciary capacity, represents both the seller and the buyer in a real estate transaction. Dual agency in Florida is not permitted.

due diligence — the exercise of an honest and reasonable degree of care in performing one's duties or obligations. A real estate agent's due diligence involves investigating the property to ensure that the property is as represented by the seller and to disclose accurate and complete information regarding the property.

due-on-sale clause — a clause in the promissory note, the security instrument, or both that states that the lender has the right to accelerate the loan if the secured property is sold or some other interest in the property is transferred.

duress — unlawful force or confinement used to compel a person to enter into a contract against his or her will.

earnest money deposit — a deposit that accompanies an offer by a buyer and is generally held in the broker's trust account.

easement — a non-possessory right to use a portion of another property owner's land for a specific purpose, as for a right-of-way, without paying rent or being considered a trespasser.

easement appurtenant — an easement that benefits, and is appurtenant to, another's land.

easement by necessity —arises as a creation of a court of law in certain cases were justice so demands, as in the case where a buyer of a parcel of land discovers that the land he or she just purchased has no access except over the land of someone other than from the person from whom the parcel was purchased.

easement in gross — an easement that benefits a legal person rather than other land.

eaves — the overhang of a roof that projects over an exterior wall of a house.

economic life — the period of time that the property is useful or profitable to the average owner or investor.

economic obsolescence — *see*, external obsolescence.

EER and SEER — Air-conditioners have an efficiency rating that states the ratio of the cooling capacity (how many BTUs per hour) to the power drawn (in watts). For room air conditioners the ratio is the EER (energy efficiency ratio); for central air conditioners the rating is the SEER (seasonal energy efficiency ratio). The higher the EER or SEER, the greater the efficiency of the air-conditioning unit. Significant savings in electricity costs can be obtained by installing more efficient air-conditioning units.

effective age — the age of an improvement that is indicated by the condition of the improvement, as distinct from its chronological age.

effective demand — demand coupled with purchasing power sufficient to acquire the property from a willing seller in a free market.

effective gross income — income from a property after an allowance for vacancies and uncollectible rents is deducted from gross income.

ejectment — a legal action to recover possession of real property from a person who is not legally entitled to possess it, such as to remove an encroachment or to evict a defaulting buyer or tenant.

emancipated minor — a minor who, because of marriage, military service, or court order, is allowed to contract for the sale or purchase of real property.

emblements — growing crops, such as grapes, avocados, and apples, that are produced seasonally through a tenant farmer's labor and industry.

eminent domain — right of the state to take, through due process proceedings (often referred to as condemnation proceedings), private property for public use upon payment of just compensation.

employee — a person who works for another who directs and controls the services rendered by the person.

employer — a person who directs and controls the services rendered by an employee.

encroachment — a thing affixed under, on, or above the land of another without permission.

encumber — To place a lien or other encumbrance on property.

encumbrance — A right or interest held by someone other than the owner the property that affects or limits the ownership of the property, such as liens, easements, licenses, and encroachments.

Endangered Species Act — a federal law that is intended to provide a means whereby the ecosystems upon which endangered species and threatened species depend may be conserved, and to provide a program for the conservation of such endangered species and threatened species.

Environmental Impact Statement (EIS) —) a written document that federal agencies must prepare for any development project that a federal agency could prohibit or regulate, and any development project for which any portion is federally financed. An EIS can include comments on the expected impact of a proposed development on such things as air quality, noise, population density, energy consumption, water use, wildlife, public health and safety, and vegetation.

Equal Credit Opportunity Act (ECOA) — a federal law that prohibits a lender from discriminating against any applicant for credit on the basis of race, color, religion, national origin, sex, marital status, or age (unless a minor), or on the grounds that some of the applicant's income derives from a public assistance program.

equal dignities rule — a principle of agency law that requires the same formality to create the agency as is required for the act(s) the agent is hired to perform.

equilibrium — the period of stability when the property changes very little.

equitable title — the right to possess and enjoy a property while the property is being paid for.

escalator clause — a provision in a lease that provides for periodic increases in rent in an amount based on some objective criteria not in control of either the tenant or the landlord, such as the Consumer Price Index.

escheat — a process whereby property passes to the state if the owner of the property dies intestate without heirs, or if the property becomes abandoned.

escrow — a neutral depository in which something of value is held by an impartial third party (called the escrow agent) until all conditions specified in the escrow instructions have been fully performed.

escrow agent — an impartial agent who holds possession of written instruments and deposits until all of the conditions of escrow have been fully performed.

escrow holder — an escrow agent

escrow instructions — the written instructions signed by all of the principals to the escrow (buyers, sellers, and lenders) that specify all of the conditions that must be met before the escrow agent may release whatever was deposited into escrow to the rightful parties.

estate — the degree, quantity, nature, duration, or extent of interest one has in real property.

estate for years — a leasehold that continues for a definite fixed period of time, measured in days, months, or years.

estate of inheritance — a freehold estate.

estoppel — a legal principle that bars one from alleging or denying a fact because of one's own previous actions or words to the contrary. Ostensible agency can be created by estoppel when a principal and an unauthorized agent act in a manner toward a third-party that leads the third party to rely on the actions of the unauthorized agent, believing that the actions are authorized by the principal.

exclusive agency listing — a listing agreement that gives a broker the right to sell property and receive compensation (usually a commission) if the property is sold by anyone other than the owner of the property during the term of the listing.

exclusive authorization and right to sell listing — a listing agreement that gives a broker the exclusive right to sell property and receive compensation (usually a commission) if the property is sold by anyone, including the owner of the property, during the term of the listing.

executed contract — a contract that has been fully performed; may also refer to a contract that has been signed by all of the parties to the contract.

executor — a person named in a will to carry out the directions contained in the will.

executory contract — a contract that has not yet been fully performed by one or both parties.

express contract — a contract stated in words, written or oral.

external obsolescence — depreciation that results from things such as (1) changes in zoning laws or other government restrictions, (2) proximity to undesirable influences such as traffic, airport flight patterns, or power lines, and (3) general neighborhood deterioration, as might result from increased crime.

Fair Housing Act — *see*, Civil Rights Act of 1968

false promise — a promise made without any intention of performing it.

Fannie Mae — a U.S. government conservatorship originally created as the Federal National Mortgage Association in 1938 to purchase mortgages from primary lenders.

federally designated targeted area — federally designated locations where homeownership is encouraged and incentivized.

fee simple absolute estate — the greatest estate that the law permits in land. The owner of a fee simple absolute estate owns all present and future interests in the property.

fee simple defeasible estate — a fee estate that is qualified by some condition that, if violated, may "defeat" the estate and lead to its loss and reversion to the grantor.

FHA — the Federal Housing Administration is a federal agency that was created by the National Housing Act of 1934 in order to make housing more affordable by increasing home construction, reducing unemployment, and making home mortgages more available and affordable.

FHFA — the Federal Housing Finance Agency is a U.S. government agency created by the Housing and Economic Recovery Act of 2008 to oversee the activities of Fannie Mae and Freddie Mac in order to strengthen the secondary mortgage market.

FICO score — a credit score created by the Fair Isaac Corporation that ranges from 300 to 850 and is used by lenders to help evaluate the creditworthiness of a potential borrower.

fiduciary relationship — a relationship in which one owes a duty of utmost care, integrity, honesty, and loyalty to another.

final map —a final map that a planning commission must approve after consideration of a tentative map before regulated subdivided property may be sold.

finder — a person who merely introduces a buyer to a seller, but does nothing else to facilitate a transaction between the buyer and seller, such as rendering assistance in negotiating terms.

fire stop — a block or board placed horizontally between studs to form a tight closure of a concealed space, thereby decreasing drafts and retarding the spread of fire and smoke.

first mortgage — a security instrument that holds first-priority claim against certain property identified in the instrument.

fixed lease — a gross lease

fixture — an object, originally personal property, that is attached to the land in such a manner as to be considered real property.

flashing — sheet metal or other material used in roof and wall construction to prevent water from entering.

flat fee listing — a listing in which the broker's compensation is a set amount rather than a percentage of the sale price.

floodplain — an area of low, flat, periodically flooded land near streams or rivers.

flue — a channel in a chimney through which flame and smoke passes upward to the outer air.

footing — concrete poured on solid ground that provides support for the foundation, chimney, or support columns. Footing should be placed below the frost line to prevent movement.

forbearance — the act of refraining from taking some action.

foreclosure — a legal process by which a lender, in an attempt to recover the balance of a loan from a borrower who has defaulted on the loan, forces the sale of the collateral that secured the loan.

foreclosure prevention alternative — a first lien loan modification or another available loss mitigation option.

Foreign Investment in Real Property Tax Act (FIRPTA) — a federal act that, with certain exceptions, requires the buyer in a real estate transaction to determine whether the seller is a non-resident alien; and if so, the buyer has the responsibility of withholding 10% of the amount realized from the sale and sending that 10% of the IRS.

four unities — refers to the common law rule that a joint tenancy requires unity of possession, time, interest, and title.

Freddie Mac — a U.S. government conservatorship originally created as the Federal Home Loan Mortgage Corporation in 1968 to purchase mortgages from primary lenders.

freehold estate — an estate in land whereby the holder of the estate owns rights in the property for an indefinite duration.

front-end ratio — the ratio of monthly housing expenses to monthly gross income.

fully amortized loan — a loan whereby the installment payments are sufficient to pay off the entire loan by the end of the loan term.

fully indexed rate — on an adjustable-rate mortgage, the index plus the margin.

functional obsolescence — depreciation that results (1) from deficiencies arising from poor architectural design, out-dated style or equipment, and changes in utility demand, such as for larger houses with more garage space, or (2) from over-improvements, where the cost of the improvements was more than the addition to market value.

gable roof — a roof with two sloping sides but not sloping ends.

gambrel roof — a roof sloped on two sides, each side having a steep lower slope and a flatter upper slope.

Garn-St. Germain Act — a federal law that made enforceability of due-on-sale provisions a federal issue.

general agent — an agent who is authorized by a principal to act for more than a particular act or transaction. General agents are usually an integral part of an ongoing business enterprise.

general lien — a lien that attaches to all of a person's nonexempt property.

general partnership — a partnership in which each partner has the equal right to manage the partnership and has personal liability for all of the partnership debts.

general plan — a comprehensive, long-term plan for the physical development of a city or county that is implemented by zoning, building codes, and other laws or actions of the local governments.

gift deed — a deed used to convey title when no tangible consideration (other than "affection") is given. The gift deed is valid unless it was used to defraud creditors, in which case such creditors may bring an action to void the deed.

Ginnie Mae — the Government National Mortgage Association is a wholly owned U.S. government corporation within HUD to guarantee pools of eligible loans that primary lenders issue as Ginnie Mae mortgage-backed securities.

goodwill — an intangible asset derived from the expectation of continued public patronage.

graduated lease — a lease that is similar to a gross lease except that it provides for periodic increases in rent, often based on the Consumer Price Index.

grantee — one who acquires an interest in real property from another.

grantor — one who transfers an interest in real property to another.

gross income — total income from a property before any expenses are deducted.

gross income multiplier (GIM) — a number equal to the estimated value of a property divided by the gross income of the property.

gross lease — a lease under which the tenant pays a fixed rental amount, and the landlord pays all of the operating expenses for the premises.

gross rent multiplier (GRM) — a number equal to the estimated value of a property divided by the gross rental income of the property.

ground lease — a lease under which a tenant leases land and agrees to construct a building or to make other significant improvements on the land.

group action — in antitrust law, two or more persons agreeing to act in a certain way.

group boycott — in antitrust law, the action of two or more brokers agreeing not to deal with another broker or brokers.

heir — a person entitled to obtain property through intestate succession.

hip roof — a sloping roof that rises from all four sides of the house.

home equity line of credit (HELOC) — a revolving line of credit provided by a home equity mortgage.

home equity mortgage — a security instrument used to provide the borrower with a revolving line of credit based on the amount of equity in the borrower's home.

Homeowner's Protection Act (HPA) — a federal law that requires lenders to disclose to borrowers when the borrowers' mortgages no longer require PMI.

homestead declaration —a recorded document that claims a particular dwelling (such as a house, condominium, boat, or mobile home) as the owner's principal place of residence and that provides limited protection for the claimant's equity in the dwelling.

homestead exemption — the amount of a homeowner's equity that may be protected from unsecured creditors.

horizontal property act — a law that provides for the creation of condominiums and establishes regulations regarding the condominiums and the condominium owners.

HUD-1 Uniform Settlement Statement — an escrow settlement form mandated by RESPA for use in all escrows pertaining to the purchase of owner-occupied residences of 1-4 dwelling units that use funds from institutional lenders regulated by the federal government.

implication — the act of creating an agency relationship by an unauthorized agent who acts as if he or she is the agent of a principal, and this principal reasonably believes that the unauthorized agent is acting as his or her actual agent.

implied contract— a contract not expressed in words, but, through action or inaction, understood by the parties.

implied easement — an easement arising by implication, as when a purchaser of mineral rights automatically acquires an implied right to enter the property to extract the minerals.

impound account — *see*, reserve account

inclusionary zoning — a zoning law that requires builders to set aside a specific portion of new construction for people of low to moderate incomes.

income approach — an appraisal approach that estimates the value of an income-producing property as being worth the present value of the future income of the property through a three-step process: (1) determine the net annual income, (2) determine an appropriate capitalization rate, and (3) divide the net income by the capitalization rate to obtain the estimate of value.

incurable depreciation — depreciation that results from (1) physical deterioration or functional obsolescence that cannot be repaired at a cost that is less than or equal to the value added to the property and (2) economic obsolescence (which is beyond the control of the property owner).

independent contractor — a person who performs work for someone, but does so independently in a private trade, business, or profession, with little or no supervision from the person for whom the work is performed.

index — under an adjustable-rate mortgage, the benchmark rate of interest that is adjusted periodically according to the going rate of T-bills, LIBOR, or the like.

innocent landowner defense — a defense to liability for cleanup of toxic waste under CERCLA (the Superfund Law) by one who acquires contaminated property after the contamination occurred and who acquired the property by inheritance or bequest or who, prior to purchasing the property, performed "all appropriate inquiries" to determine that the property had not been contaminated.

installment note — a promissory note in which periodic payments are made, usually consisting of interest due and some repayment of principal.

installment sale — a sale in which the seller receives at least one payment in a later tax period and may report part of the gain from the sale for the year in which a payment is received.

integration — the growth and development stage of property.

intentional misrepresentation — the suggestion, as a fact, to a party that which is not true committed by another party who does not believe it to be true and who makes the suggestion with the intent to deceive the first party, who was deceived to his or her detriment, such as by being induced to enter into a contract.

interest — the compensation fixed by the parties for the use of money.

interest-rate cap — under an adjustable-rate mortgage, the maximum that the interest rate can increase from one adjustment period to the next or over the life of the entire loan.

interpleader — an action that allows for a neutral third party (such as a real estate agent) to avoid liability to two or more claimants (such as a seller and buyer) to the same money or property (such as an earnest money deposit) by forcing the claimants to litigate among themselves, letting the court determine who deserves what while not enmeshing the neutral third party in the litigation.

Interstate Land Sales Full Disclosure Act — a federal consumer protection act that requires that certain land developers register with the Consumer Financial Protection Bureau if they offer across state lines parcels in subdivisions containing 100 or more lots. Subdivisions where each lot in the subdivision contains at least 20 acres are exempt from this registration requirement. A developer must provide each prospective buyer with a Property Report that contains pertinent information about the subdivision and that discloses to the prospective buyer that he or she has a minimum of 7 days in which to rescind the purchase agreement.

intestate — not having made, or not having disposed of by, a will.

intestate succession — transfer of the property of one who dies intestate.

inverse condemnation — as provided for in Florida Statutes, 70.001, a judicial action brought by a landowner to force the condemnation of the landowner's land where nearby condemned land or land used for public purposes (such as for noisy airports) severely reduces the value of the landowner's land.

involuntary lien — a lien created by operation of law, not by the voluntary acts of the debtor.

jamb — the vertical sides of a door or window that contact the door or sash.

joint ownership — ownership of property by two or more persons.

joint tenancy —a form of joint ownership which has unity of possession, time, interest, and title.

joist — one of a series of parallel heavy horizontal timbers used to support floor or ceiling loads.

Jones v. Mayer — a landmark 1968 United States Supreme Court case that held that the Civil Rights Act of 1866 was constitutional and that the Act prohibited all racial discrimination, whether private or public, in the sale or rental of property.

judicial foreclosure — a foreclosure carried out not by way of a power-of-sale clause in a security instrument, but under the supervision of a court.

judgment — a court's final determination of the rights and duties of the parties in an action before it.

jumbo loan — a mortgage loan the amount of which exceeds conforming loan limits set by the FHFA on an annual basis.

junior mortgage — a mortgage that, relative to another mortgage, has a lower lien-priority position.

land contract — a real property sales contract.

land installment contract — a real property sales contract.

lateral support — the support that soil receives from the land adjacent to it.

lease extension — a continuation of tenancy under the original lease.

lease-option — a lease (also referred to as a lease with an option to purchase) that provides the tenant with the right, but not the obligation, to purchase the leased property at a specified price within a specified period of time.

lease-purchase — an agreement (also referred to as a lease with an obligation to purchase) that provides for the purchase of property preceded by a lease under which a portion of each lease payment is applied to the purchase price.

lease renewal — a continuation of tenancy under a new lease.

leasehold estate — a less-than-freehold estate.

legatee — one who acquires personal property under a will.

lessee — a person (the tenant) who leases property from another.

lessor — a person (the landlord) who leases property to another.

less-than-freehold estate — an estate in which the holder has the exclusive right to possession of land for a length of time. The holder of a less-than-freehold estate is usually referred to as a lessee or tenant.

level payment note — a promissory note under which all periodic installment payments are equal.

leverage — a method of multiplying gains (or losses) on investments by using borrowed money to acquire the investments.

license to use —a personal right to use property on a nonexclusive basis. A license to use is not considered an estate.

lien —an encumbrance against real property that is used to secure a debt and that can, in most cases, be foreclosed.

lien priority — the order in which lien holders are paid if property is sold to satisfy a debt.

lien stripping — a method sometimes used in Chapter 13 bankruptcies to eliminate junior liens on the debtor's home.

lien theory — a legal theory of mortgage, holding that the mortgagor retains both legal and equitable title of the property, including exclusive possession and use of the property. The mortgagee simply possesses a lien against the property (usually a lien of higher priority than certain other liens, such as judgment liens). Upon default, the mortgagee must go through a formal (judicial) foreclosure proceeding to obtain legal title and possession.

life estate — a freehold estate the duration of which is measured by the life of a natural person — either by the life of the person holding the estate, or by the life or lives of one or more other persons.

limited liability partnership — a partnership in which there is at least one general partner and one or more limited partners. The limited partners have no liability beyond their investment in and pledges to the partnership.

lintel — a horizontal support made of wood, stone, concrete, or steal that lies across the top of a window or door and supports the load above.

liquidated damages — a sum of money that the parties agree, usually at the formation of a contract, will serve as the exact amount of damages that will be paid upon a breach of the contract.

lis pendens — (Latin for "action pending") a notice of pendency of action.

listing agreement — a written contract between a real estate broker and a property owner (the principal) stipulating that in exchange for the real estate broker's procuring a buyer for the principal's property, the principal will compensate the broker, usually with a percentage of the selling price.

loan flipping — the practice of frequently refinancing loans that result in little more than the generation of additional loan fees.

loan modification — a restructuring or modification of a mortgage or deed of trust on terms more favorable to the buyer's ability (or desire) to continue making loan payments.

loan servicing — the administration of a loan from the time the loan proceeds are dispersed to the time the loan is paid off in full.

loan-to-value ratio (LTV) — the amount of a first mortgage divided by the lesser of (1) the appraised value of the property or (2) the purchase price of the property.

long-term capital gain — the capital gain on the sale of a capital asset that was held for a relatively long period of time, usually more than one year.

lot, block, and tract land system — (see " recorded map or plat system ")

maker — the person who makes a promissory note.

margin — a number of percentage points, usually fixed over the life of the loan, that is added to the index of an adjustable-rate mortgage to arrive at the fully indexed rate.

market allocation — in antitrust law, the process of competitors agreeing to divide up geographic areas or types of products or services they offer to customers.

market price — the price actually paid for a particular property.

market value — as defined for appraisal purposes by HUD/FHA is: "The most probable price which a property should bring in a competitive and open market under all conditions requisite to a fair sale, the buyer and seller, each acting prudently, knowledgeably and assuming the price is not affected by undue stimulus."

material fact — a fact that is likely to affect the decision of a party as to whether to enter into a transaction on the specified terms.

mechanics lien — a specific lien claimed by someone who furnished labor or materials for a work of improvement on real property and who has not been fully paid.

median price per square foot — the median price per square foot of a set of properties is the price per square foot of the property whose price per square foot is such that half of the properties in the set have an equal or lower price per square foot and half have an equal or higher price per square foot.

Megan's Law — an informal name for various federal and state laws that provide for the registration of sex offenders and for the making available to the public information regarding the location of these offenders.

menace — a threat to commit duress or to commit injury to person or property.

meridians — (see and compare "base lines")

metes and bounds land description — a method of describing a parcel of land that uses physical features of the locale, along with directions and distances, to define the boundaries of the parcel.

moldings — patterned strips, usually of wood, used to provide ornamental finish to cornices, bases, windows, and door jambs.

mortgage banker — a primary lender that uses its own money in creating a mortgage loan.

mortgage broker — an individual or company that finds borrowers and matches them with lenders for a fee.

mortgagee — a lender or creditor to whom a mortgagor gives a mortgage to secure a loan or performance of an obligation.

mortgage loan originator (MLO) — a person who takes, or offers to take, a residential mortgage loan application or offers or negotiates terms of a residential mortgage application for compensation or gain or in expectation of compensation or gain.

mortgagor — the borrower who gives a mortgage on his or her property to secure a loan or performance of an obligation.

mudsill — for houses built on a concrete slab, the wood sills that are bolted to all sides of the slab, providing a means of attaching portions of the framing for the house to the foundation.

multiple listing service — an organization (MLS) of real estate brokers who share their listings with other members of the organization.

mutual consent — refers to the situation in which all parties to a contract freely agree to the terms of the contract; sometimes referred to as a "meeting of the minds."

National "Do Not Call" Registry — a registry established by the Federal Trade Commission to protect consumers from unwanted commercial telephone solicitations.

National Association of Real Estate Brokers — a real estate trade association whose members are called Realtists®.

National Association of Realtors® — the largest real estate trade association in the United States, founded in 1908, whose members are called Realtors®.

National Environmental Policy Act (NEPA) — a federal law intended to protect, and to promote the enhancement of, the environment.

negative amortization — a loan repayment scheme in which the outstanding principal balance of the loan increases because the installment payments do not cover the full interest due.

negative amortized loan (NegAm loan) — a loan by which the installment payments do not cover all of the interest due — the unpaid part of the interest due being tacked onto the principal, thereby causing the principal to grow as each month goes by.

negative covenant — a contractual promise not to do certain acts, such as build a fence on a property, the remedy for breach thereof being either monetary damages or injunctive relief, not forfeiture.

negative fraud — the act of not disclosing a material fact which induces someone to enter into a contractual relationship and that causes that person damage or loss.

negligent misrepresentation — an assertion not warranted by the information of the party making the assertion that an important fact was true, which was not true, relied on by another party to that party's detriment.

net income — income from a property remaining after expenses are deducted from gross income.

net lease — a lease under which the tenant pays a fixed rental amount plus some of the landlord's operating expenses.

net listing — a listing agreement providing the broker with all proceeds received from the sale over a specified amount. Net listings are not legal in many states.

NMLS — the Nationwide Mortgage Licensing System and Registry is a mortgage licensing system developed and maintained by the Conference of State Bank Supervisors and the American Association of Residential Mortgage Regulators for the state licensing and registration of state-licensed loan originators.

nonconforming loan — a loan not in conformance with FHFA guidelines.

nonconforming use — a zoning exception for areas that are zoned for the first time or that are rezoned and where established property uses that previously were permitted to not conform to the new zoning requirements. As a general rule, such existing properties are "grandfathered in," allowing them to continue the old use but not to extend the old use to additional properties or to continue the old use after rebuilding or abandonment.

non-judicial foreclosure — a foreclosure process culminating in a privately conducted, publicly held trustee's sale. The right to pursue a non-judicial foreclosure is contained in the power-of-sale clause of a mortgage or deed of trust, which, upon borrower default and the beneficiary's request, empowers the trustee to sell the secured property at a public auction.

notice of default (NOD) — a document prepared by a trustee at the direction of a lender to begin a non-judicial foreclosure proceeding.

notice of pendency of action — a notice that provides constructive notice to potential purchasers or encumbrancers of a piece of real property of the pendency of a lawsuit in which an interest in that piece of real property is claimed.

notice of sale — a document prepared by a trustee at the direction of a lender that gives notice of the time and place of sale of an identified foreclosed property.

novation — a substitution of a new obligation or contract for an old one, or the substitution of one party to a contract by another, relieving the original party of liability under the contract.

nuisance — anything that is indecent or offensive to the senses, or an obstruction to the free use of property, so as to interfere with the comfortable enjoyment of life or property.

offer — a proposal by one person (the offeror) to enter into a contract with another (the offeree).

offeree — one to whom an offer to enter into a contract is made.

offeror — one who makes an offer to enter into a contract.

open listing — a listing agreement that gives a broker the nonexclusive right to sell property and receive compensation (usually a commission) if, but only if, the broker is the first to procure a buyer for the property.

opinion of title — a written rendering of an opinion on the condition of ownership of title in a real estate transaction prepared by an attorney after examination of an abstract of title.

option contract — a contract that gives the purchaser of the option the right to buy or lease a certain property at a set price any time during the option term.

ordinary interest — interest calculated by the 30/360 day count convention.

origination fee — the fee a lender charges to cover expenses of processing a loan, such as purchasing credit reports, inspection reports and appraisals, and paying office expenses and salaries of personnel who interview borrowers and analyze the reports and appraisals.

ostensible agency — an agency in which the principal intentionally, or by want of ordinary care, causes a third person to believe another to be his agent who was not actually employed by him.

parol evidence rule — a rule of evidence that prohibits the introduction of extrinsic evidence of preliminary negotiations, oral or written, and of contemporaneous oral evidence, to alter the terms of a written agreement that appears to be whole.

partially amortized loan — an installment loan under which monthly payments pay all of the interest due but not enough of the principal to fully pay off the loan at the end of the loan term. In such a case, a balloon payment would be due at the end of the loan term.

partial release clause — a clause in a blanket mortgage that allows a developer to sell off individual parcels and pay back, according to a release schedule, only a proportionate amount of the blanket loan.

partition —a court-ordered or voluntary division of real property held in joint ownership into parcels owned in severalty.

passive income — in general, income from either rental activity or from a business in which the taxpayer does not materially participate.

passive investor — an investor who does not actively contribute to the management of the business invested in.

patent, land — an instrument used to convey government land.

payee — the person to whom a promissory note is made out.

payment cap —under an adjustable-rate mortgage, the maximum amount that installment payments may increase from one adjustment period to the next or over the life of the loan.

percentage lease — a lease, often used in shopping centers, under which the tenant typically pays a base rent amount plus a percentage of the gross receipts of the tenant's business.

period of redemption — a period of time after a sheriff's sale in a judicial foreclosure proceeding during which the borrower may redeem his or her property by paying off the entire debt plus costs.

periodic tenancy — an estate from period to period.

physical deterioration — depreciation that results from wear and tear of use and from natural causes.

physical life — the period of time that the property lasts with normal maintenance.

pitch — the degree of inclination or slope of a roof.

plaintiff — the one who brings a lawsuit.

plaster — a mixture of lime or gypsum, sand, water, and fiber that is applied to walls and ceilings and that hardens into a smooth coating.

point of beginning — the fixed starting point in the metes and bounds method of land description.

point — in finance, a point is equal to 1% of the loan amount. The term is used by lenders to measure discount charges and other costs such as origination fees and private mortgage insurance premiums.

police power — the power of a government to impose restrictions on private rights, including property rights, for the sake of public welfare, health, order, and security, for which no compensation need be made.

portfolio loans — loans that primary lenders retain in their own investment portfolios rather than sell into the secondary market.

post-dated check — a check dated with a date after the date the check is written and signed.

potentially responsible party — as defined by the EPA, anyone who ever owned or operated a contaminated property, as well as anyone who produced the waste, transported the waste to the property, or disposed of the waste on the property.

power of attorney — a special written instrument that gives authority to an agent to conduct certain business on behalf of the principal. The agent acting under such a grant is sometimes called an attorney in fact.

power-of-sale clause — a clause contained in most trust deeds that permits the trustee to foreclose on, and sell, the secured property without going to court.

preapproval —an evaluation of a potential borrower's ability to qualify for a loan that involves a credit check and verification of income and debt of the potential borrower.

predatory lending — the imposition of unfair, deceptive, abusive, or fraudulent loan terms on borrowers.

prepayment penalty — a fee charged to a borrower for paying off the loan faster than scheduled payments call for.

prequalification — an initial unverified evaluation of a potential borrower's ability to qualify for a mortgage loan.

prescription — a method of acquiring an interest in property by use and enjoyment for five years.

prescriptive easement — an easement acquired by prescription.

price fixing — an agreement between competitors to set prices or price ranges.

price per square foot — the price per square foot of a specific property is determined by dividing the price (either selling or listing) by the property's square footage. Appraisers determine the square footage of a property by using the *outside* measurement of the property.

primary financing — first mortgage property financing.

primary lender — lenders who originate mortgage loans.

primary mortgage market — the market where mortgage loans are originated.

principal — the one whom an agent represents in a fiduciary capacity.

principle of anticipation — principle that value is derived from a calculation of anticipated future benefits to be derived from the property, not from past benefits, though past benefits may inform as to what might be expected in the future.

principle of balance — principle that the maximum value of property, its highest and best use, is created and maintained when land use by interacting elements of production are in equilibrium or balance.

principle of change — principle that property values are in a constant state of flux due to economic, environmental, political, social, and physical forces in the area.

principle of competition — principle that increased competition results in increased supply in relation to demand, and thereby to lower profit margins.

principle of conformity — principle that the maximum value of land is achieved when there is a reasonable degree of social, economic, and architectural conformity in the area.

principle of contribution — principle that improvements made to a property will contribute to its value or that, conversely, the lack of a needed improvement will detract from the value of the property.

principle of four-stage life cycle — principle that property goes through a process of growth, stability, decline, and revitalization.

principle of plottage — states that assembling two or more parcels of land into one parcel results in the larger parcel having a greater value than the sum of the values of the smaller parcels.

principle of progression — principle that the value of a residence of less value tends to be enhanced by proximity to residences of higher value.

principle of regression — principle that the value of a residence of higher value tends to be degraded by the proximity to residences of lower value.

principle of substitution — principle that the value of a property will tend toward the cost of an equally desirable substitute property.

principle of supply and demand — principle that the value of property in a competitive market is influenced by the relative levels of supply and demand: the greater level of demand in relation to the level of supply, the greater the value.

principle of the highest and best use — principle that the best use of a property in terms of value is the use most likely to produce the greatest net return (in terms of money or other valued items).

private mortgage insurance (PMI) — mortgage insurance that lenders often require for loans with an LTV more than 80%.

privity of contract — a legal doctrine that states that a legally enforceable relationship exists between the persons who are parties to a contract.

privity of estate — a legal doctrine that states that a legally enforceable relationship exists between the parties who hold interests in the same real property.

probate — a legal procedure whereby a superior court in the county where the real property is located or where the deceased resided oversees the distribution of the decedent's property.

procuring cause — a common law legal concept developed by the courts to determine the proportioning of commissions among agents involved in a real estate transaction In general, an agent who is a procuring cause of a sale originated a chain of events that resulted in the sale and is thereby entitled to at least some part of the total commission generated by the sale.

profit á prendre — the right to enter another's land for such purposes as to drill for oil, mine for coal, or cut and remove timber.

promissory note — a contract whereby one person unconditionally promises to pay another a certain sum of money, either at a fixed or determinable future date or on demand of the payee.

property disclosure statement — a statement filled out by the seller of residential property consisting of 1 to 4 dwelling units, disclosing to potential purchasers defects in the property that are known to the seller, or that should be known to the seller upon reasonable inspection.

proration — an adjustment of expenses that either have been paid or are in arrears in proportion to actual time of ownership as of the closing of escrow or other agreed-upon date.

protected class — a group of people protected from discrimination by federal or state law.

protection clause — *see*, safety clause.

public dedication — a gift of an interest in land to a public body for public use, such as for a street, a park, or an easement to access a beach.

public grant — public land conveyed, usually for a small fee, to individuals or to organizations, such as to railroads or universities.

puffing — the act of expressing a positive opinion about something to induce someone to become a party to a contract.

purchase money loan — a deed of trust or mortgage on a dwelling for not more than four families given to a lender to secure repayment of a loan which was in fact used to pay all or part of the purchase price of that dwelling, occupied entirely or in part by the purchaser.

pyramid roof a hip roof that has no ridge.

quantity survey method — the most detailed method of estimating the replacement or reproduction cost of a structure, in which an estimate is made of the cost of all of the raw materials needed to replace the building. Such material-cost information is available in construction cost handbooks

quiet title action — *see*, suit to quiet title

quitclaim deed — a deed that contains no warranties of any kind, no after-acquired title provisions, and provides the grantee with the least protection of any deed; it merely provides that any interest (if there is any) that the grantor has in the property is transferred to the grantee.

rafter — one of a series of parallel sloping timbers that extend from the ridgeboard to the exterior walls, providing support for the roof.

ratification —the act of creating an agency relationship by a principal who accepts or retains the benefit of an act made by an unauthorized agent.

real estate investment trust (REIT) — a company that invests in and, in most cases operates, income-producing real estate and that meets numerous criteria, such as the necessity of being jointly owned by at least 100 persons.

real estate owned (REO) — property acquired by a lender through a foreclosure sale.

real estate professional — a real estate investor who (1) materially participates for at least 750 hours during the tax year in the real estate business and (2) spends more than 50% of his or her personal services performed in all businesses during the tax year in the real estate business that he or she materially participates in.

Real Estate Settlement Procedures Act (RESPA) — a federal law designed to prevent lenders, real estate agents, developers, title insurance companies, and other agents (such as appraisers and inspectors) who service the real estate settlement process from providing kickbacks or referral fees to each other, and from facilitating bait-and-switch tactics.

real property sales contract — an agreement in which one party agrees to convey title to real property to another party upon the satisfaction of specified conditions set forth in the contract and that does not require conveyance of title within one year from the date of formation of the contract.

Realtist® — a member of the National Association of Real Estate Brokers.

Realtor® — a member of the National Association of Realtors®.

reconciliation — the process of ascertaining value by comparing and evaluating values obtained from comparables or from different valuation approaches; the process of comparing what is in a trust fund account with what should be in the account.

reconveyance deed — a deed executed by the trustee of a deed of trust after the promissory note is paid off in full by the borrower and the lender instructs the trustee to so execute the reconveyance deed, which reconveys legal title to the borrower

recorded map or plat system — a method of land description that states a property's lot, block, and tract number, referring to a map recorded in the county where the property is located.

rectangular survey system — a method of land description based on a grid system of north-south lines ("ranges") and east-west lines ("tier" or "township" lines) that divides the land into townships and sections.

red flag — a condition that should alert a reasonably attentive person of a potential problem that warrants further investigation. Examples include stains on ceilings or walls, the smell of mold, and warped floors or walls.

redlining — the illegal practice of refusing to make loans for real property in particular areas.

Regulation Z — the set of regulations that implement the Truth-in-Lending Act (TILA).

reinforced concrete — concrete poured around steel bars or metal netting to increase its ability to withstand tensile, shear, and compression stresses.

rejection — the act of an offeree that terminates an offer. An offer may be rejected (1) by submitting a new offer, (2) by submitting what purports to be an acceptance but is not because it contains a variance of a material term of the original offer, or (3) by express terms of rejection.

rejuvenation — the phase when a property is rebuilt, remodeled, or otherwise revitalized to a new highest and best use.

reliction — a natural process by which the owner of riparian or littoral property acquires additional land that has been covered by water but has become permanently uncovered by the gradual recession of water.

remainder — the residue of a freehold estate where, at the end of the estate, the future interest arises in a third person.

remainder depreciation — depreciation that will occur after the date of valuation.

remainderman — a person who inherits or is entitled to inherit property held as a life estate when the person whose life determines the duration of the life estate passes away.

replacement cost — the cost of replacing improvements with those having equivalent utility, but constructed with modern materials, designs, and workmanship.

reproduction cost — the cost of replacing improvements with exact replicas at current prices.

request for a reconveyance — an instrument that a lender sends to a trustee requesting that the trustee execute and record a deed of reconveyance that is then sent to the borrower.

rescission — the cancellation of a contract and the restoration of each party to the same position held before the contract was entered into.

reserve account — in reference to loan servicing, the escrow account from which the loan servicer typically pays, on behalf of the borrower, property taxes, hazard insurance, and any other charges (such as mortgage insurance) with respect to the loan.

residual value — an estimate of the reasonable fair market value of a property at the end of its useful life.

respondeat superior — in agency law, the doctrine that a principal is liable for the acts of an agent if those acts were performed within the scope of the agent's authority. (See, vicarious liability.)

retaliatory eviction — an eviction action brought to retaliate against a tenant for making a habitability complaint or for asserting other of the tenant's legal rights.

return on investment (ROI) — an investor's cash flow (net income minus financing charges) divided by the investor's actual cash investment (as distinct from the purchase price).

reverse mortgage — a security instrument for a loan for homeowners over the age of 62 who have a large amount of equity in their homes, usually designed to provide such homeowners with monthly payments, often over the lifetime of the last surviving homeowner who either moves out of the house or dies.

reversion — the residue of a freehold estate where at the end of the estate, the future interest reverts to the grantor.

revocation — the withdrawal of an offer by the person who made the offer.

rezoning amendment — an amendment to a zoning ordinance that property owners may request if they feel that their area has been improperly zoned.

ridgeboard — a horizontal board placed on edge at the apex of a roof to which the upper ends of the rafters are attached.

right of first refusal — the right to be given the first chance to purchase a property at the same price, terms, and conditions as is offered to third parties if and when the property is put up for sale.

right of survivorship — the right to succeed to the interest of a joint tenant or, if community property with right of survivorship, to succeed to the interest of a spouse or registered domestic partner. Right of survivorship is the most important characteristic of joint tenancy.

riparian rights — the rights of a landowner to use water from a stream or lake adjacent to his or her property, provided such use is reasonable and does not injure other riparian owners.

robocall — a pre-recorded, auto-dialed telephone call.

root of title — any title transaction purporting to create or transfer the estate claimed by any person and which is the last title transaction to have been recorded at least 30 years prior to the time when marketability is being determined. The effective date of the root of title is the date on which it was recorded.

R-value — a measure of the resistance of insulation to heat transfer. The FTC requires sellers of new homes to disclose the R-value of each home's insulation. The higher the R-value, the greater is the effectiveness of the insulation.

SAFE Act — the Safe and Fair Enforcement for Mortgage Licensing Act of 2008 was designed to improve consumer protection and reduce mortgage fraud by setting minimum standards for the licensing and registration of mortgage loan originators.

safety clause — a provision in a listing agreement, providing that the broker will earn the full commission if the property is sold within a specified number of days after the termination of the listing to a buyer with whom the broker has dealt in certain specified ways regarding the property.

sales comparison approach — an appraisal approach that compares recent sales of similar properties in the area to evaluate the market value of the subject property.

salesperson — a natural person who is employed by a licensed real estate broker to perform acts that require having a real estate license.

salvage value — residual value.

sandwich lease — a leasehold interest that lies between a primary lease and a sublease.

sash — frames that contain one or more windowpanes.

scarcity — a lack of abundance.

scrap value — residual value.

second mortgage — a security instrument that holds second-priority claim against certain property identified in the instrument.

secondary financing — second mortgage and junior mortgage property financing

secondary mortgage market — the market where mortgages are sold by primary mortgage lenders to investors.

secret profit — any compensation or beneficial gain realized by an agent not disclosed to the principal. Real estate agents must always disclose any interest that they or their relatives have in a transaction and obtain their principals' consent.

section — one square mile, containing 640 acres.

security instrument — the written instrument by which a debtor pledges property as collateral to secure a loan.

SEER — (see EER)

self-help eviction — a landlord's denial of possession of leased premises to a tenant without complying with the legal process of eviction.

seller carry back loan — a loan or credit given by a seller of real property to the purchaser of that property.

senior mortgage — a mortgage that, relative to another mortgage, has a higher lien-priority position.

separate property — property that is owned in severalty by a spouse or registered domestic partner. Separate property includes property acquired before marriage or the registering of domestic partnership, and property acquired as a gift or by inheritance during marriage or registered domestic partnership.

servient tenement — land that is burdened by an easement.

setback — a designation of a governing body as to how far a structure must be situated from something else, such as a curb or a neighboring property.

settlement — *see*, closing

severalty — ownership of property by one person.

severance — the act of detaching an item of real property that changes the item to personal property, such as the cutting down of a natural tree. Also, the act of terminating a relationship, such as the act of partitioning by court order for the transfer of an interest that changes a joint tenancy into a tenancy in common.

severance damages — damages paid to an owner of land partially taken by eminent domain where the value of the remaining portion of the owner's land is severely reduced by the severance of the condemned a portion of owner's land.

sheriff's deed — a deed given at the foreclosure of a property, subsequent to a judgment for foreclosure of a money judgment against the owner or of a mortgage against the property. A sheriff's deed contains no warranties and transfers only the former owner's interest in the property.

sheriff's sale — a sale of property following a judicial foreclosure.

Sherman Act — the federal law passed in 1890 that prohibits agreements, verbal or written, that have the effect of restraining free trade.

short sale — a pre-foreclosure sale made by the borrower (usually with the help of a real estate agent) with lender approval of real estate for less than the balance due on the mortgage loan.

short-term capital gain — the capital gain on the sale of a capital asset that was held for a relatively short period of time, usually one year or less.

sill — the board or metal forming the lower side of the frame for a window or door; the lowest part of the frame of a house, resting on the foundation and providing the base for the studs.

simple interest — the type of interest that is generated only on the principal invested.

single agent — an agent who represents only one party in a given transaction.

single point of contact — an individual or team of personnel employed by a mortgage loan servicer, each of whom has the ability and authority to assist a borrower in assessing whether the borrower may be able to take advantage of a foreclosure prevention alternative offered by, or through, the mortgage servicer.

situs — the legal location of something; also refers to the preference for a particular location to live, work, or invest in

special agent — an agent for a particular act or transaction.

special assessment — a tax levied against properties in a particular area that are benefited by improvements such as for streets, water, and sewers.

specific lien — a lien that attaches only to specific property.

specific performance — a court order that requires a person to perform according to the terms of a contract.

spot zoning —refers to the zoning of isolated properties for use different from the uses specified by existing zoning laws. To spot zone a particular property may, in some cases, be a violation of the requirement that police power apply similarly to all property similarly situated, which in turn arises from the constitutional guarantee of equal protection under the law.

square-foot method — the most widely used method of estimating reproduction or replacement cost of a building, involving the collection cost data on recently constructed similar buildings and dividing the total cost by the square footage to obtain cost per square foot

standard subdivision — is a subdivision with no common areas of ownership or use among the owners of the subdivision parcels.

standby loan commitment — a commitment by a lender to make a take-out loan after construction on a property is completed

statute of frauds — a law that requires certain types of contracts, including most real estate contracts, to be in writing and signed by the party to be bound in order for the contract to be enforceable.

statute of limitations — a law that requires particular types of lawsuits to be brought within a specified time after the occurrence of the event giving rise to the lawsuit.

steering — the illegal practice of directing people of protected classes away from, or toward, housing in particular areas.

stigmatized property — a property having a condition that certain persons may find materially negative in a way that does not relate to the property's actual physical condition.

straight note — a promissory note under which periodic payments consist of interest only.

straight-line depreciation — the expensing of a property by equal amounts over the useful life of the property, determined by subtracting from the cost of the property the estimated residual value of the property and dividing that amount by the useful life of the property measured in years.

straight-line method — a method of calculating annual depreciation of an improvement by dividing the cost of the improvement by the estimated useful life of a typical such improvement.

strict foreclosure — a foreclosure process permitted in a few states, whereby no public sale of the property is made — full title simply passes to the lender.

subagent — an agent of an agent.

subjacent support — the support that soil receives from land beneath it.

subject to — acquiring real property that is burdened by a mortgage without becoming personally liable for the mortgage debt.

subjective value — (also referred to as *value in use*) is value placed on the amenities of a property by a specific person.

sublease — a transfer of a tenant's right to a portion of the leased premises or to the entire premises for less than the entire remaining lease term.

subordination clause — a provision in a mortgage or deed of trust that states that the mortgage or deed of trust will have lower priority than a mortgage or deed of trust recorded later.

subrogation — the substitution of one party for another in regard to pursuing a legal right, interest, or obligation. Subrogation is a legal right used by insurance companies to acquire the right from a policyholder to sue in the place of the policyholder for damages the insurance company paid to the policyholder for some act committed by a third party.

tacking — the adding of time periods of use or possession of land by successive persons to satisfy the number of years required to obtain a prescriptive easement or ownership of property by adverse possession.

take-out loan — a loan that provides long-term financing for a property on which a construction loan had been made.

tax assessor — the county or city official who is responsible for appraising property.

tax auditor — the county or city official who maintains the county tax rolls.

tax collector — the county or city official who is responsible for collecting taxes.

tax deed — the deed given to the successful buyer at a tax sale. A tax deed conveys title free and clear from private liens, but not from certain tax liens or special assessment liens, or from easements and recorded restrictions.

tenancy at sufferance — a tenancy that arises when a lessee holds over after the termination of a lease, the term of which is limited, without renewing the lease.

tenancy at will — a tenancy without a specific duration, such as from year to year or from month to month, that may be terminated by either party giving proper written notice.

tenancy by the entirety — recognized in some states, a special form of joint tenancy between a married couple, in which, as in a joint tenancy, there is the right of survivorship, but in which, unlike in a joint tenancy, neither spouse may convey his or her interest in the property during the lifetime of the other spouse without the consent of the other spouse.

tenancy for years — see, estate for years.

tenancy in common — a form of joint ownership that is presumed to exist if the persons who own the property are neither married nor registered domestic partners and they own undivided interests in property. Tenants in common may hold unequal interests; however, if the deed does not specify fractional interests among the tenants, the interests will be presumed to be equal.

tenancy in partnership — a form of joint ownership in which the partners combine their assets and efforts in a business venture.

tenancy with a specific duration — see, estate for years.

tenancy without a specific duration — *see*, tenancy at will.

term loan — see, straight loan.

testament — a will.

testator — one who dies leaving a will.

title plant — a duplicate of county title records maintained at title insurance companies for use in title searches.

title search — an examination of all relevant public documents to determine whether there exist any potential defects (such as judicial liens, lis pendens, or other encumbrances, including tax liens and special assessments) against the title.

title theory — a legal theory of mortgage, holding that a mortgage transfers legal title to the mortgagee (the lender) while the mortgagor (the borrower) retains equitable title to the property, which permits the mortgagor exclusive possession and use of the property. Upon default, the mortgagee is entitled to immediate possession and use (such as to collect rents) of the property.

township — six square miles, containing 36 sections.

trade fixtures — objects that a tenant attaches to real property for use in the tenant's trade or business. Trade fixtures differ from other fixtures in that, even though they are attached with some permanence to real property, they may be removed at the end of the tenancy of the business.

transactional broker — In Florida, a transactional broker provides limited representation to a buyer, a seller, or both, in a real estate transaction, but does not represent either in a fiduciary capacity or as a single agent, and neither the buyer nor the seller is responsible for the acts of a transactional broker. However, in most states that permit transactional broker status, a transactional broker is considered to be a nonagent who brings the parties to a real estate transaction together and lets the parties do all of the negotiating among themselves. All states that provide for transactional broker status impose an obligation on the transactional broker to act fairly, honestly, and competently to find qualified buyers or suitable properties, but the transactional broker does not owe fiduciary legal obligations to any of the parties.

transferability — the ability to transfer some interest in property to another.

triggering term — any of a number of specific finance terms stated in an advertisement for a loan that triggers Regulation Z disclosure requirements in the advertisement.

triple net lease — a lease under which the tenant pays a fixed rent plus the landlord's property taxes, hazard insurance, and all maintenance costs.

trust account — an account set up by a broker at a bank or other recognized depository in the state where the broker is doing business, into which the broker deposits all funds entrusted to the broker by principles or others.

trust deed — a three-party security device, the three parties being the borrower (trustor), the lender (beneficiary), and a third-party (trustee*)* to whom "bare legal title" is conveyed.

trust fund overage — a situation in which a trust fund account balance is greater than it should be.

trust fund shortage — a situation in which a trust fund account balance is less than it should be.

trustee — a person who holds something of value in trust for the benefit of another; under a deed of trust, a neutral third-party who holds naked legal title for security.

trustor — a borrower who executes a deed of trust.

Truth-in-Lending Act (TILA) — a federal consumer protection law that was enacted in 1968 with the intention of helping borrowers understand the costs of borrowing money by requiring disclosures about loan terms and costs (in particular, the APR) and to standardize the way in which certain costs related to the loan are calculated and disclosed.

tying arrangement — occurs in antitrust law when the seller conditions the sale of one product or service on the purchase of another product or service.

underwriter — one who analyzes the risk of, and recommends whether to approve, a proposed mortgage loan.

undivided interest — an ownership interest in property in which an owner has the right of possession of the entire property and may not exclude the other owners from any portion by claiming that a specific portion of the property is his or hers alone.

unenforceable contract — a contract that a court would not enforce.

Uniform Commercial Code (UCC) — a set of laws that established unified and comprehensive regulations for security transactions of personal property and that superseded existing laws in that field.

unilateral contract — a contract in which one party gives a promise that is to be accepted not by another promise but by performance.

unit-in-place method — a method of estimating the replacement or reproduction cost of a structure by calculating the unit cost of components of the structure.

universal agent — an agent given power of attorney to act on behalf of a principal for an unlimited range of legal matters.

unlawful detainer — a legal action to regain possession of real property.

useful life — the estimated period during which a property generates revenue (if the property is an income property) or usefulness (if the property, such as a private residence, has value other than income value).

U.S. government survey system — see rectangular survey system

usury — the charging of interest in excess of that allowed by law.

utility — the usefulness of property; its ability to satisfy a potential buyer's need or desire, such as to provide shelter or income.

VA — the Department of Veterans Affairs is a federal agency designed to benefit veterans and members of their families.

valid contract — a contract that is binding and enforceable in a court of law.

value — the present worth to typical users or investors of all rights to future benefits, arising out of property ownership.

variance — an exception that may be granted in cases where damage to the value of a property from the strict enforcement of zoning ordinances would far outweigh any benefit to be derived from enforcement.

vendee — the purchaser in a real property sales agreement

vendor — the seller in a real property sales agreement.

void contract — a purported contract that has no legal effect.

voidable contract — a contract that, at the request of one party only, may be declared unenforceable, but is valid until it is so declared.

voluntary lien — a lien obtained through the voluntary action of the one against whose property the lien attaches.

warranty of habitability — mandated by both statutes and by common law, an implied warranty in any residential lease that the premises are suitable for human habitation.

wetlands — as defined by the EPA, "areas that are soaked or flooded by surface or groundwater frequently enough or for sufficient duration to support plants, birds, animals, and aquatic life. Wetlands generally include swamps, marshes, bugs, estuaries, and other inland and coastal areas, and are federally protected."

will — a document that stipulates how one's property should be distributed after death; also called a testament.

writ — a court order commanding the person to whom it is directed to perform an act specified therein.

writ of attachment — a writ ordering the seizure of property belonging to a defendant to ensure the availability of the property to satisfy a judgment if the plaintiff wins.

writ of execution — a writ directing a public official (usually the sheriff) to seize and sell property of a debtor to satisfy a debt.

writ of possession — a court order that authorizes the sheriff or other eviction authority to remove a tenant and the tenant's possessions from leased premises.

zoning — laws of a city or county that specify the type of land-use that is acceptable in certain areas.

REAL ESTATE MATH

Section 1: Basic Math Concepts

The only math you are expected to know for the real estate exam is the basic math that will help you solve practical, everyday real estate problems. Memorize a few measurement correspondences, become familiar with a few simple equations and how they apply to practical real estate problems, and you will do just fine.

Here are the measurement correspondences that you should memorize:

- 1 mile = 5,280 feet or 320 rods
- 1 rod = 16½ ft.
- 1 township = 6 mi.× 6 mi. = 36 sections
- 1 section = 1 mi. × 1 mi. = 640 acres
- 1 acre = 43,560 square feet

Converting Decimals, Percentages, and Fractions. Being able to calculate percentages and fractions is of vital importance to real estate agents because commissions, property taxes, interest rates, buyer qualification ratios, loan-to-value ratios, capitalization rates, and gross rent and gross income multipliers all involve working with percentages and fractions.

To convert a percentage to a decimal, simply remove the % sign and move the decimal point two places to the left:

15% → .15

74.6% → .746

To convert a decimal to a percent, move the decimal point two places to the right and add the % sign:

.75 → 75%

1.12 → 112%

To convert a fraction to a decimal, divide the numerator (the number on top) by the denominator (the number on the bottom):

1/5→ 1÷ 5 → .20

3/4→ 3 ÷ 4→ .75

A. Area:

When calculating the area of something (usually expressed in square feet), remember that the area of a rectangle is base × height and the area of a triangle is ½ × base × height.

Example: *Kevin is going to purchase the lot shown in Figure 10 below and build on it a house and garage, also shown in Figure 10. He has been quoted the following: $150 per square foot for the house; $40 per square foot for the garage; $10 per square foot for the land. What is the total amount that Kevin will pay for this lot, house, and garage?*

Answer: First we calculate the square footage of each item:

house area = 60' × 30' = 1,800 ft.²

garage area = 25' × 18' = 450 ft.²

lot area = ½ × 100' × 150' = 7,500 ft.²

cost of house = 1800 ft.² × $150 per ft.² = $270,000

cost of garage = 450 ft.² × $40 per ft.² = $18,000

cost of the lot = 7500 ft.² × $10 per ft.² = $75,000

Total = $363,000

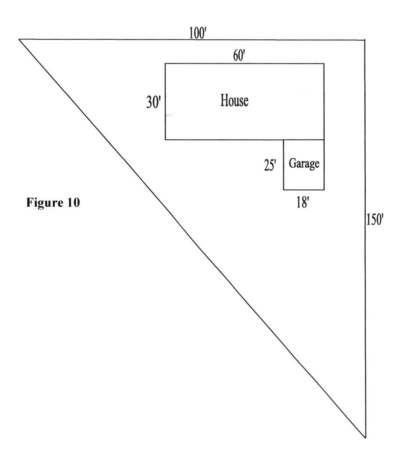

Figure 10

Example: The SW¼ of the SW¼ of the NW¼ of section 10 of Baker Township contains how many square feet?

42

Answer: A section of a township contains 640 acres. Therefore, ¼ × ¼ × ¼ × 640 acres = 10 acres. Because there are 43,560 square feet per acre, we get 435,600 square feet.

B. Loan-to-Value Ratios:

The ***loan-to-value ratio (LTV)*** is an important risk factor lenders use to assess the viability of a proposed loan. LTV is defined as the amount of a first mortgage divided by the *lesser* of (1) the appraised value of the property or (2) the purchase price of the property. As a general rule, a high LTV (usually seen as over 80%) will either cause:

- the loan to be denied;
- the lender to increase the cost of the loan to the borrower; or
- the lender to require that the borrower pay for private mortgage insurance.

Example: For a property with an appraised value of $100,000, a sales price of $110,000, and a loan of $90,000, the LTV would be $90,000/$100,000 = 90%.

Example: *If a loan has an LTV of 80%, an appraised value of $120,000, and the sales price of $110,000, what is the amount of the loan?*

Answer: LTV = .8 = loan amount/$110,000.

Therefore, loan amount equals $110,000 × .8 = $88,000.

C. Discount Points:

In finance, a point is equal to 1% of the loan amount. The term is used by lenders to measure charges and other costs such as origination fees and private mortgage insurance premiums. If 1.25 points are charged on a $150,000 loan, the lender would collect 1.25% of $150,000, or $1,875.

Example: *Suppose that Sally is purchasing a house for $250,000 with 20% down. The lender requires 2.5 discount points. How much will Sally pay the lender for the discount points?*

Answer: The loan amount is $250,000 - $50,000 (the down payment) = $200,000.

$200,000 × .025 = $5,000

D. Equity:

Equity is the difference between the current market value of a property and the total indebtedness against the property. If each mortgage payment pays all of the current interest plus some part of the outstanding principal, then the equity increases with each mortgage payment in the amount of the outstanding principal reduction due to the mortgage payment.

Example: Suppose that you have a home with a fair market value $300,000, a first mortgage with outstanding principal of $200,000, and a home equity loan with outstanding principal of $27,000. The equity in your home would be ($300,000 - $200,000) - $27,000 = $73,000.

Home equity loans and home equity lines of credit (HELOC) are loans and lines of credit based on the equity of your home. Typically, these kinds of loans give a loan (or credit line) up to 80% of the appraised value of your home, minus total outstanding indebtedness against the home.

Example: *Joe's home is appraised that $200,000. The first mortgage against his home has an outstanding balance of $100,000. Joe has just arranged to obtain an 80% home equity line of credit of the type described above. What is the amount of his line of credit?*

Answer: ($200,000 × .8) - $100,000 = $60,000.

Note that the answer is NOT ($200,000 - $100,000) × .8 = $80,000.

E. Down Payment/Amount to Be Financed:

A down payment is the amount of money that a lender requires a purchaser to pay toward the purchase price. Note that a down payment is what a lender requires; an earnest money deposit is what a seller requires. The two are different, though an earnest money deposit is often applied toward the down payment.

Example: Andrew is purchasing a home with a purchase price of $300,000 and an appraised value of $290,000. If the lender is willing to loan 80% of the lesser of the purchase price and the appraised value, how much will be Andrew's down payment?

Answer: Loan amount = $290,000 × .8 = $232,000.

Down payment = purchase price - loan amount = $300,000 - $232,000 = $68,000.

Section 2: Calculations for Transactions, Including Mortgage Calculations

Installment loans require periodic payments that include some repayment of principal as well as interest. Installment loans are the most common type of loan used to finance real estate, and the most frequently used installment loan is the *level payment loan* — a loan under which all periodic installment payments are equal, though the amount allocated to principal and interest may vary over the term of the loan. A loan wherein the payments are sufficient to pay off the entire loan by the end of the loan term is referred to as a *fully amortized loan*.

Example: *José purchased a home for $195,130 with a 6% fixed-rate, fully amortized 30-year loan in the principal amount of $156,104. He makes payments of $936 per month. What is the amount of unpaid principal on this loan after the first month's payment?*

Answer: $156,104 × .06 ÷ 12 = $780.52 (first month's interest)

$936 - $780.52 = $155.48 (first month's principal payment)

$156,104 - $155.48 = $155,948.52 (principal balance after first month's payment).

Section 3: Property Tax Calculations

Property taxes are assessed on an *ad valorem* (according to value) basis. The value used is not necessarily the fair market value; rather, it is the assessed value. To find the annual property tax, take the assessed value, subtract any applicable exemption (such as a homestead exemption), and multiply by the annual tax rate.

Example: *A home has a fair market value of $450,000, a homestead exemption of $75,000, an assessed value of $368,000, and a county property tax of 1.2%. What is the annual county property tax on this home?*

Answer: ($368,000 - $75,000) × .012 = $3,516.

Example: *In the above example, what is the amount of tax savings due to the homestead exemption?*

Answer: $75,000 × .012 = $900.

Section 4: Prorations (utilities, rent, property taxes, insurance, etc.)

When calculating proration problems, it is important to know what *day count convention* to use. An exact calculation would take into account the precise number of days: 30 days for some months, 31 or 28 or 29 for other months; 365 days for some years, 366 for leap years. In the days before computers, such calculations would have been quite burdensome, so the *30/360 day count convention* was adopted to simplify certain calculations. When using the 30/360 day count convention, each month is considered to have 30 days, and each year is considered to have 360 days. A year consisting of 360 days with 12 months of 30 days each is often referred to as a *statutory year*, or a *banker's year*. The 30/360 day count convention for calculating *proration, interest, insurance premiums*, and similar expenses is standard in the real estate market. However, in some areas, rules for calculating proration, interest, etc., are based on the actual number of days in a month or year.

Proration questions that appear on your real estate exam will state whether calculations should be based on 360 or 365 days a year, and whether the day of closing belongs to the seller or to the buyer.

A. Commission and Commission Splits:

Because nearly every real estate agent expects to receive commissions (many, hopefully!), it is not unlikely that a question or two relating to commissions might appear on an exam.

Example: *Jessica is a real estate salesperson who found a buyer for a home that sold for $800,000. Jessica's employing broker received a 5% commission for the sale. The agreement between the broker and Jessica provides that she receive 40% of the broker's commission on every sale she procures. What is Jessica's commission on this transaction?*

Answer: Here the solution is to first find the broker's commission:

5% of $800,000 = .05 × $800,000 = $40,000. Jessica is to receive 40% of $40,000 = .40 × $40,000 = $16,000.

Another way to think about such a problem is to note that Jessica receives 40% of 5% = .40 × .05 = .02 = 2% of the sales price. Using this 2% figure, we find that 2% of $800,000 = .02 × $800,000 = $16,000.

Example: *Bob is a salesperson who works for broker Janet. Bob's agreement with Janet is that he gets a commission of 40% of whatever commission Janet receives on sales made by Bob. Bob procures a sale of a house that was listed by broker Susan, who had a cooperating agent agreement with Janet to split the commission on the sale 50-50. Susan's listing agreement with the owner called for a 6% commission. Bob's commission on the sale was $6,000. How much did the house sell for?*

45

Answer: Because they tend to be long-winded, these types of problems *appear* to involve much more thought than they actually do — they simply need to be approached methodically, step-by-simple-step, until the answer falls out:

The problem tells us that:

$6,000 = 40\%$ of 50% of 6% of Sales Price

$\quad\quad = (.4 \times .5 \times .06) \times$ Sales Price

$\quad\quad = .012 \times$ Sales Price (i.e., 1.2% of Sales Price)

Therefore, dividing each side of the equation by .012, we get

$500,000 =$ Sales Price.

B. Seller's Proceeds of Sale:

As a general rule, at the close of escrow in a real estate transaction certain allocations of expenses incurred in the ordinary course of property ownership must be made. For example, if the escrow closes midyear or midmonth, the seller may have prepaid taxes, insurance, or association dues, in which case credit to the seller's account should be made. Conversely, if the seller is behind on paying taxes or insurance, etc., the seller's account should be debited. Such an adjustment of expenses that either have been paid or are in arrears in proportion to actual time of ownership as of the closing or other agreed-upon date is called **proration**. Proration, like ordinary interest, is generally calculated according to the 30/360 day count convention (statutory year).

To compute proration, follow these steps:

1. determine which, if any, expenses are to be prorated;
2. determine to whom the expenses should be credited or debited;
3. determine how many days the expenses are to be prorated;
4. calculate the per day proration amount; and
5. multiply the number of days by the per day proration amount.

Example 12: *Susan purchased a condo for $200,000 that had been rented from Bob at $1,500 a month. Escrow closed on September 16. How should the $200,000 selling price be adjusted at close of escrow if the day of closing belongs to the buyer?*

Answer: Rent is normally collected *in advance* on the first day of the month, so unless stated otherwise one should make this assumption in proration of rent problems. Under this assumption, Bob received $1,500 on or about September 1, but only deserved to keep half of the month's rent because Susan acquired ownership of the condo on September 16. Therefore, Susan should be credited $750 at the close of escrow.

C. Transfer Tax/Conveyance Tax/Revenue Stamps:

Many states tax the transfer of real estate. These taxes are variously referred to as transfer taxes, conveyance taxes, or stamp taxes and are usually imposed either (1) on the total amount of the transfer price (usually less the amount of a loan or other liens the seller had on the property that the buyer assumes responsibility for paying), or (2) imposed on the amount of either assumed mortgages or newly created mortgages.

Example: *A residential property was purchased for $450,000. The state documentary transfer fee is $.55 for each $500 or fraction thereof. The property was purchased with*

$400,000 cash and an assumption of the $50,000 seller's mortgage. Assumed mortgages are exempt from the transfer fee in this state. What is the documentary transfer fee?

Answer: $400,000 = $500 × 800.

800 × $0.55 = $440.

D. Amortization Tables:

Although interest and principal payments for loans are now calculated on financial calculators or on calculation software freely available on the Internet, we will look briefly at a simplified amortization table to get a feel for how such a chart was used (in the old days) to calculate the monthly payments for fixed-rate loans at various interest rates. (See Figure 11).

The table displays in the left column the interest rate, and in columns to the right, the term in years of a fixed-rate, fully amortized loan. To find the monthly payment *per $1,000* principal borrowed, simply find the intersection of the rate and term of the loan.

Fig. 11

Monthly Payment Per $1,000 on Fixed-Rate, Fully Amortized Loans				
Rate	10-year term	15-year term	30-year term	40-year term
4%	10.125	7.397	4.775	4.180
5%	10.607	7.908	5.369	4.822
6%	11.102	8.439	5.996	5.503
7%	11.611	8.989	6.653	6.215
8%	12.133	9.557	7.338	6.954

Example: *Susan makes payments of $936 per month, including 6% interest on a fixed-rate, fully amortized 30-year loan. What was the initial amount of her loan?*

Answer: Finding where 6% and a 30-year term intersect in the table, we obtain the number 5.996 which is the dollar amount per month per $1,000 of the initial loan.

$5.996/$1,000 = $936/loan amount. Therefore,

loan amount = ($936 ÷ $5.996) × $1,000 = $156,104.

E. Interest Rates:

Interest is the "rent" we pay to possess, use, and enjoy someone else's money. The yearly rent for each dollar we use (borrow) is called the interest rate — if we pay 8¢ each year for each dollar, the interest rate is 8% per year.

Interest problems generally involve four simple concepts:

1. *Interest Rate* (which, to avoid wordiness, we will call Rate);

47

2. *Principal* (the amount of money borrowed);

3. *Time* (the number of years or fraction of years the principal is borrowed);

4. *Interest Due and Owing* (which we will call Interest).

Because the interest due and owing (Interest) is equal to the interest rate (Rate) times the amount of money borrowed (Principal) times the amount of time the money is borrowed (Time),

Interest = Rate × Principal × Time

The above formula is known as **simple interest**, which considers interest to be generated only on the principal invested. A more rapid method of generating interest earnings is referred to as compounding. **Compound interest** is generated when accumulated interest is reinvested to generate interest earnings from previous interest earnings. Though the amount of interest generated can be revved up by compounding yearly, semiannually, quarterly, daily, or even continuously, real estate exams stick with simple interest, as do most real estate loans on which interest is paid monthly. Interest calculated by the 30/360 day count convention is referred to as **ordinary interest**.

Example: *If $6,000 is loaned for one 30-day month on the basis of simple interest, and the total amount of principal and interest due at the end of that month is $6,017.5, what annual rate of interest was charged?*

Answer: $17.50 (interest) = $6,000 (principal) × (annual interest rate/12).
Therefore, annual interest rate = ($17.50 ÷ $6,000) × 12 = 3.5%

F. Interest Amounts:

Example: *What is the interest on a $400,000 loan for 1 year, 2 months, and 10 days at 6% interest (using a statutory year)?*

Answer: The time elapsed is 360 days + 60 days + 10 days = 430 days.
430 ÷ 360 = 1.19444 years. Therefore, applying our formula
Interest = Rate × Principal × Time, we get
Interest = .06 × $400,000 × 1.19444 = $28,666.56.

Example: *Jessica borrows $12,000 from her friend Susan. The terms of the loan are that principal will be paid back in equal monthly installments over a five-year period along with the interest that was generated at the annual rate of 6% during the month on the outstanding balance of principal owing. What is Jessica's payment to Susan at the end of the second month?*

Answer: To answer this question, we first have to answer another question; namely, how much principal does Jessica pay Susan at the end of the first month? This is due to the fact that Susan's first month payment will reduce the principal amount on which the second month payment must be calculated.

Because there are 60 months in 5 years, the amount of Susan's monthly payment attributable to principal is $12,000 ÷ 60 = $200. Therefore, the amount of principal owed after the first-month payment is made is $12,000 - $200 = $11,800. Consequently, the second month payment will be $200 + the interest due on $11,800 *for one month*. Because the interest rate is 6% annually, the monthly rate is 1/2%. Thus, the second-month payment is $200 + 1/2% of $11,800 = $259.

G. Monthly Installment Payments:

To obtain the monthly mortgage payment on a level payment loan, the amount of principal and interest is obtained from a loan table (or from a financial calculator) and to this is added 1/12 of the annual property taxes and 1/12 of the home insurance to obtain the PITI (principal, interest, tax, and insurance) payment.

Example: *John and Sandra make monthly mortgage payments of $725.68 for principal and interest. Their annual property taxes are $1,245.30 and their homeowner's insurance is $217 per year. What is their monthly PITI payment?*

Answer: $1,245.30 ÷ 12 = $103.78 tax per month

$217 ÷ 12 = $18.08 insurance per month

Total PITI payment per month = $725.68 + $103.78 + $18.08 = $847.54.

H. Buyer Qualification Ratios:

Prior to approving a loan, a loan processor must obtain information on monthly housing expenses, which the underwriter will use to establish a ratio of monthly housing expenses to monthly gross income, and information on total monthly recurring debt obligations, which the underwriter will use to establish a ratio of total monthly expenses to monthly gross income. Monthly housing expenses include principal, interest, taxes, and insurance (referred to as **PITI**). Total monthly expenses include housing expenses plus additional long-term monthly debt service, such as for car payments, credit card payments, child support, and alimony. In this context, "long-term debt" typically refers to debt that is not scheduled to be retired within 9 months. Monthly housing expenses divided by the monthly gross income is referred to as the **PITI** or **front-end ratio**. Total monthly expenses divided by monthly gross income is referred to as the **LTD** or **back-end ratio**.

For example, suppose that

- monthly gross income = $4,000;
- PITI = $1,000; and
- additional long-term monthly debt expenses = $400.

In this case,

- PITI ratio = $1,000 ÷ $4,000 = 25%
- LTD ratio = $1,400 ÷ $4,000 = 35%

Example: *Sam and Susan's combined monthly gross income is $6,000. What is the maximum PITI they can have to qualify if the lender demands no greater than a 32% PITI ratio?*

Answer: $6,000 × .32 = $1,920.

I. Prepayment Penalties:

A prepayment penalty is a fee charged to a borrower for paying off a loan faster than scheduled payments call for. The penalty is usually calculated as a percentage of a certain number of months of interest on the loan. Therefore, if the borrower has a $200,000 loan with interest at the rate of 4%, and the prepayment penalty is 80% of six months interest, the prepayment payment would be $80\% \times 4\%/\text{year} \times \frac{1}{2} \text{ year} \times \$200,000 = \$3,200$.

Section 5: Calculations for Valuation

A. Competitive/Comparative Market Analyses (CMA):

We discussed in Chapter 3, Section 3, some of the differences between a comparative market analysis (also referred to as a competitive market analysis) (CMA) and the sales comparison approach to appraisal. However, both the sales comparison approach and a CMA compare in the same manner recent sales of similar local properties to arrive at an estimated market value of a subject property. A detailed example of the sales comparison approach can be found in Chapter 3, Section 2, Figure 5.

The most important thing to keep in mind in a sales comparison appraisal or in a CMA problem is that it is *the values of items of the comparable properties, not the value of items of the subject property, that are adjusted* for differences between the comparables and the subject property. The second most important thing to keep in mind is that if a comparable property has a *superior* feature (such as a better pool) the value of the comparable is adjusted *down* in the amount of the difference between the value of the comparable pool and the value of the subject property pool. On the other hand, had the value of the comparable pool been *less* than the value of the subject pool, the value of the comparable property would have been adjusted *up* accordingly.

Example: *The subject property and a comparable are tract homes that share a common wall. The two houses appear almost exactly the same except that the comparable has an inferior view estimated to be worth $3,000 less than the subject view, and the comparable has superior landscaping estimated to be worth $4,500 more than the subject landscaping. What adjustments should be made?*

Answer: The comparable has a view and landscaping combined value of $1,500 more than the subject view and landscaping value. Therefore, the comparable value should be adjusted down by $1,500.

B. Net Operating Income:

Net operating income (NOI) is determined as follows:

a) estimate the potential annual gross income the property;

b) deduct from the gross income an annual allowance for vacancies and uncollectible rents to arrive at the ***effective gross income***; and

c) deduct from the effective gross income the estimate of annual operating expenses, including fixed expenses (such as hazard insurance and real estate taxes), maintenance, and reserves for replacements of building components.

Not all expenses are deducted from effective gross income to obtain net operating income. Examples of such expenses include mortgage payments and taxes on income.

Example: *What is the value of a property based on the following information?*

Estimated potential annual gross income: $95,000

Vacancies and uncollectible rents: 7%

Annual maintenance expenses and utilities: $10,000

Annual property taxes: $9,500

Annual insurances: $1,500

Capitalization rate: 9.5%

Answer: $95,000 × .07 = $6,650 (vacancy and uncollectible rents losses)

$95,000 - $6,650 = $88,350 (effective gross income)

$88,350 - $21,000 (operating expenses) = $67,350 (NOI)

$67,350 ÷ .095 = $708,947 (rounded).

C. Depreciation:

Although many different ways to calculate depreciation are allowed by law (depending on what law one has to satisfy), the only method of depreciation that appears to be tested on real estate license exams is **straight-line depreciation**, which assumes that the property depreciates by an *equal amount* each year.

Depreciation is based on what is considered the **useful life** (also referred to as the **economic life**) of the property and on the estimated **residual value** (also referred to as **salvage value** or **scrap value**) of the property at the end of the property's useful life. Some property, such as computers, have a much shorter useful life than do buildings, so it is always important when considering depreciation to know what the useful life of the item being depreciated is. Straight-line depreciation is defined as:

Annual Depreciation = (Cost of Property - Residual Value) ÷ (useful life in years).

Thus, if the property has a 5-year useful life and no residual value, the rate of (straight-line) depreciation is 100% ÷ 5 years = 20% per year.

Example: *Evan purchases a building for $3,000,000 that has a useful life of 30 years and salvage value of $0. After 10 years, what is the value of the building, if by "value" we mean the original cost less accumulated straight-line depreciation?*

Answer: Here the depreciation rate is: 100% ÷ 30 years = 3⅓ % per year.

3⅓ % per year × 10 years = 33⅓ % depreciation.

33⅓ % of the initial value = 33⅓ % × $3 million = $1 million.

Therefore, value = cost - depreciation = $2,000,000.

Example: If in the above example the land the building was on was worth $750,000, and the question asked for the value of the property after 10 years, the answer would be $2,750,000.

D. Capitalization Rate:

The *capitalization rate* (also referred to as the *cap rate*) is the rate that an appraiser estimates is the yield rate expected by investors from comparable properties in current market conditions. To estimate the capitalization rate of a certain property, an appraiser will collect data on the market value of comparable properties, on the vacancies and uncollectible rents of these comparable properties, and on the operating expenses of these comparable properties. Then, because value = net operating income ÷ capitalization rate, the capitalization rate can be calculated for these comparable properties as net operating income ÷ market value.

Example: *If the annual net operating income of a property is $20,000 and the capitalization rate is 8.5% per year, what would be the value of the property based on an income valuation of the property?*

Answer: $20,000 ÷ 8.5% = $235,294 (rounded).

E. Gross Rent and Gross Income Multipliers (GRM, GIM):

As we have seen, the income approach uses capitalization of *net* operating income to arrive at the valuation of a property. However, some investors, especially of single-family homes, use a simpler method of determining value: capitalization of *gross* income. If only gross rents are capitalized, this approach to value is called the *gross rent multiplier (GRM)* approach; if additional income is involved (such as from parking fees), the method is called the *gross income multiplier (GIM)* approach.

Example: *Using the gross rent multiplier approach, suppose the sales price of a condo is $1,400,000 and the monthly rent is $5,000. What is the monthly gross rent multiplier of this condo?*

Answer: In this case the sales price is $1,400,000 ÷ $5,000 = 280 times the monthly rental; i.e., the monthly gross rent multiplier is 280.

Example: Suppose now that other comparable homes in the area have a monthly gross rent multiplier similar to the home in the prior example. Further, suppose that a comparable home in the area with a fair market value of $900,000 is to be rented. Using the gross rent multiplier approach, what would be the monthly rent for this subject property.

Answer: By dividing the value ($900,000) by the monthly gross rent multiplier (280), we calculate a rent of $3,214 per month.

PRACTICE EXAM #1:

Abbreviations used in this Practice Exam are:

DBPR — Department of Business and Professional Regulation
FAC — Florida Administrative Code
FREC — Florida Real Estate Commission
FS — Florida Statutes

1. The license of any sales associate who does not complete the postlicensure education requirement prior to the first renewal following initial licensure

a. Is placed on inactive status

b. Will be suspended

c. Is null and void

d. Will be impounded within 30 days of the end of the first biennial term of the license.

2. Which of the following is an example of personal property?

a. A trade fixture

b. A bookcase bolted to a family library wall

c. The tree growing in the backyard of a single-family home

d. A carpet that was custom cut to fix a particular living room

3. Florida Statutes, Chapter 475, does not exempt which of the following individuals and/or entities from holding a real estate license?

a. An owner of one or part of one or more timeshare periods for the owner's own use and occupancy who later offers one or more of such periods for resale.

b. Any person acting as an attorney in fact for the purpose of the execution of contracts.

c. Any employee of a brokerage office who performs real estate services on behalf of the brokerage provided the employee is paid a straight salary.

d. Any property management firm or any owner of an apartment complex for the act of paying a finder's fee or referral fee to an unlicensed person who is a tenant in such apartment complex provided the value of the fee does not exceed $50 per transaction.

4. A point of beginning is a necessary feature of the

a. U.S. government survey system

b. Metes and bounds system

c. Rectangular survey system

d. Recorded plat system

5. In the Florida Statutes, the term "plat" refers to

a. A written statement sworn to under penalty of perjury before a public official, such as a notary public

b. The conveyance of title or other interest in real property

c. Concrete poured on solid ground that provides support for the foundation, chimney, or support columns of a structure

d. A map or delineated representation of the subdivision of lands

6. The selling price of the home Lisa is purchasing $275,000. The lender is willing to loan 80% of the lesser of the purchase price or the appraised value. If the amount the lender is willing to loan is $220,000, what is the appraised value of Lisa's home?

a. $270,000

b. $250,000

c. $265,000

d. None of the above

7. Which of the following does *not* represent an exception to "first to record, first in right"?

a. Real estate taxes

b. Judgment liens

c. Subordination agreements

d. Special assessments

8. An easement that benefits not land but a specific legal person is called

a. A servient easement

b. A dominant easement

c. An easement appurtenant

d. An easement in gross

9. If a licensee changes the licensee's business address, the Florida Real Estate Commission must be notified within how many days of the change of address?

a. 5

b. 7

c. 10

d. 15

10. Which of the following is not true about a corporation?

a. It may be a joint tenant

b. It may be a tenant in common

c. It may have ownership in severalty

d. It may have joint ownership

11. A thing that starts out as personal property but then is attached to the land in such a manner as to be considered real property is

a. A trade fixture

b. An emblement

c. An encroachment

d. A fixture

12. Which of the following statements is (are) true?

a. Under certain circumstances, a Florida real estate broker may be issued multiple licenses.

b. Under certain circumstances, a Florida real estate sales associate may be issued multiple licenses.

c. Under certain circumstances, a Florida real estate broker associate may be issued multiple licenses.

d. All of the above are true.

13. Public limitations on private property include

a. Eminent domain

b. CC&Rs

c. Deed restrictions

d. Habendum

14. The primary purpose of escheat is to

a. Help ensure public health and safety

b. Raise revenue for transportation related expenses

c. Prevent property from remaining ownerless or abandoned

d. Raise revenue for the state treasury

15. A school is permitted to build in an area zoned exclusively for single-family homes. This is an example of

a. Spot zoning

b. Conditional use

c. Variance

d. Nonconforming use

16. Unless a customer involved in a Florida real estate transaction agrees otherwise in writing, any Florida real estate broker involved in the transaction

a. Is presumed to be a single agent

b. Is presumed to be a transaction broker

c. Is presumed to be involved in a non-brokerage relationship with the customer

d. Is presumed to be a designated agent

17. Under the Superfund Law, short-term responses to a perceived imminent threat that requires a prompt response are called

a. Removal actions

b. Remedial actions

c. Responsible party actions

d. Contamination actions

18. Covenants, conditions, and restrictions (CC&Rs) generally are _____ whereby persons agree to limit certain things, such as the color of paint on houses or the type of architecture used to build or remodel houses.

a. Negative covenants

b. Affirmative covenants

c. Negative conditions

d. Affirmative conditions

19. Arnold sells Bob a parcel of land "on condition" that the land never be used to sell alcoholic beverages. Two years later, Bob builds a retail building on the site, obtains a license to sell alcoholic beverages, and subsequently begins selling wine and beer at the site. Who may bring an action for forfeiture of title against Bob?

a. Arnold

b. The zoning commission

c. The state alcoholic beverages board

d. The county Board of Supervisors

20. The Florida Brokerage Relationship Disclosure Act requires that

a. Transaction brokerage relationships must be disclosed in writing when dealing with residential real estate transactions

b. No brokerage relationships must be disclosed in writing when dealing with residential real estate transactions

c. Single agency relationships must be disclosed in writing when dealing with nonresidential real estate transactions

d. None of the above

21. A desert city passes a zoning ordinance that prohibits swimming pools containing more than a certain number of cubic meters of water. Susan's pool is considerably larger than the new zoning ordinance allows, but she is told by the zoning board that she may keep her pool. This is an example of

a. Nonconforming use

b. Spot zoning

c. Conditional use

d. Inclusionary zoning

22. Joel paid $285,000 for his house. This $285,000 represents the _____ of Joel's house.

a. Market value

b. Market price

c. Utility value

d. Function value

23. The value of a high-quality home will be lessened by proximity to smaller, lower-quality homes by the principle of

a. Conformity

b. Regression

c. Plottage

d. Contribution

24. Which appraisal approach determines the market value of the subject property by capitalizing the estimated future income of the property?

a. Market data approach

b. Replacement cost approach

c. Income approach

d. Summation approach

25. Margaret is a broker who has assigned her sales associate Susan to represent as a single agent the buyer, and her sales associate Jonathan to represent the seller as a single agent, in a nonresidential real estate transaction. Each of the following statements is false except

a. Jonathan owes fiduciary duties to the buyer.

b. The combined assets of the buyer and the seller must be $1 million or more.

c. Margaret has definitely placed herself an illegal dual agency relationship with the buyer and the seller.

d. Each of the above statements is false.

26. When using the sales comparison approach to appraisal,

a. If a feature of a comparable is inferior to the same type of feature in the subject property, then the difference in value of features is added to the comparable property

b. If a feature of a comparable is inferior to the same type of feature in the subject property, then the difference in value of features is subtracted from the comparable property

c. Similar properties that were sold through short sales are used

d. Similar properties that were sold at foreclosure sale are used

27. A real estate licensee owes to a potential seller or buyer with whom the licensee has no brokerage relationship each of the following duties, except

a. Confidentiality

b. Dealing honestly and fairly

c. Disclosing all known facts that materially affect the value of the residential real property which are not readily observable to the buyer

d. Accounting for all funds entrusted to the licensee

28. For appraisal purposes, depreciation is

a. Defined as the increase in value due to any cause

b. Referred to as book depreciation

c. Defined as the loss in value due to any cause

d. Referred to as functional obsolescence

29. The return on investment (ROI) of a property is calculated by

a. Dividing the investor's cash flow (net income minus financing charges) by the investor's actual cash investment

b. Dividing the annual net income by the purchase price of the property

c. Dividing the purchase price of the property by the annual net income

d. Dividing the annual gross income by the purchase price of the property

30. One of the significant risks taken by the leveraged investor is

a. That property values will rise

b. That interest rates will remain constant

c. That insurance rates will remain constant

d. Negative cash flow

31. Pursuant to Florida real estate law, which of the following statements is false?

a. When advertising on a site on the Internet, the brokerage firm name must be placed adjacent to or immediately above or below the point of contact information.

b. A broker's main office may be in a residential location, if not contrary to local zoning ordinances, provided the minimum office requirements are met and the required broker's sign is properly displayed.

c. When the licensee's personal name appears in the advertisement, at the very least the licensee's last name must be used in the manner in which it is registered with the FREC.

d. Each active broker must maintain an office, consisting of at least two enclosed rooms in a building of stationary construction.

32. Which of the following statements is false?

a. A preliminary title report identifies the property with an assessor's parcel number, street address, and legal description.

b. A preliminary title report identifies the current owner of the residence.

c. A preliminary title report includes an appraisal of the property.

d. A preliminary title report reveals title policy exceptions, such as property taxes, assessments, encumbrances, liens, and easements.

33. In an adjustable-rate mortgage, the fully indexed rate is

a. Equal to the index minus the margin

b. Equal to the index plus the margin

c. Often referred to as a teaser rate

d. Often referred to as an adjustment rate

34. What is the minimum age at which a person qualifies for a reverse mortgage?

a. 55

b. 60

c. 62

d. 65

35. Benefits of FHA-insured loans do not include

a. Lower FICO scores are required than are typically required by conventional loans

b. Relatively low loan amounts insured

c. The loans are assumable upon approval by the FHA

d. Relatively lenient PITI ratios

36. A sales associate who receives a good-faith deposit from a potential buyer must deliver the deposit to the sales associate's broker or employer no later than the end of the

a. Day of receipt of the item to be deposited

b. Next business day following receipt of the item to be deposited

c. Second business day following receipt of the item to be deposited

d. Third business day following receipt of the item to be deposited

37. A defeasance clause states

a. The amount to be charged to a borrower for paying off the loan faster than scheduled payments call for

b. That when the loan debt has been fully paid, the lender must release the property from the lien so that legal title free from the lien will be owned by the borrower

c. That the mortgage or deed of trust will have lower priority than a mortgage or deed of trust recorded later

d. That the purchaser agrees to be primarily liable on a loan that was taken out by the seller

38. John signed a buyer's agency agreement with broker Bob. In relation to John, Bob is a

a. Specific agent

b. Single agent

c. Special agent

d. General agent

39. Charles is a sales associate who receives on Thursday a good-faith deposit from a potential buyer for the purchase of a condo. Charles delivered the good-faith deposit to his broker, Kathy, the next business day, Friday. Assuming no holidays during the following week, Kathy must deposit the good-faith deposit Charles received no later than the end of

a. Monday

b. Tuesday

c. Wednesday

d. Thursday

40. What kind of agency is created when a principal intentionally, or by want of ordinary care, causes a third person to believe another to be his agent who is not actually employed by the principal?

a. Ostensible

b. Universal

c. Mistaken

d. Designated

41. There is a rule of equity known as _____ that holds that one who causes another to rely on his or her words or actions shall be prohibited from later taking a contrary position detrimental to the person who so relied.

a. Estoppel

b. Ratification

c. Express agreement

d. The equal dignities rule

42. Which of the following statements is false?

a. A designated agent is an agent authorized by a real estate broker to represent a specific principal to the exclusion of all other agents in the brokerage.

b. A subagent is an agent who represents only one party in a given transaction.

c. A universal agent is an agent given power of attorney to act on behalf of a principal for an unlimited range of legal matters.

d. Ostensible agency is created when a principal intentionally, or by want of ordinary care, causes a third person to believe another to be his agent who is not actually employed by the principal.

43. Which of the following statements is (are) true?

a. Under certain circumstances, a broker is allowed to place escrow funds in an interest-bearing account.

b. A broker is allowed to place escrow funds in an interest-bearing account only after obtaining written permission from all parties to the transaction.

c. A broker is allowed to place escrow funds in a non-interest-bearing account.

d. All of the above statements are true.

44. Placing funds belonging to clients or customers into accounts also holding the agent's funds is considered

a. Conversion

b. Commingling

c. Reconciliation

d. Trust fund accounting

45. An agency relationship cannot be terminated by force of law because of

a. Bankruptcy

b. Change in law

c. Steep drop in the value of real estate

d. Loss of license

46. If a broker supplies financing to build a house with the stipulation that the broker will have the listing to sell the house,

a. The broker's appointment as the agent is irrevocable

b. The seller may terminate the listing because agency is a personal relationship based on trust and confidence

c. The seller may terminate the agency because of the conflict of interest

d. The broker is what is referred to as a designated agent

47. If no funds are entrusted to a broker during a real estate transaction, for how long must the broker preserve at least one legible copy of all books, accounts, and records pertaining to his or her brokerage business from the date of execution by any party of any listing agreement, offer to purchase, rental property management agreement, rental or lease agreement, or any other written or verbal agreement which engages the services of the broker?

a. 7

b. 5

c. 3

d. 1

48. Amanda has the listing for a single-family house. Susan is interested in purchasing the house and goes to visit Amanda at Amanda's office to discuss the property's details. Amanda should not disclose to Susan that

a. The heater in the house needs to be replaced

b. The guestroom was added without a required permit

c. The seller is willing to accept a somewhat lower price than listed

d. The roof leaks over one of the bedrooms, which isn't used by the current owner

49. The seller of a residential dwelling unit built before 1978 must

a. Pay for an inspection of the dwelling unit

b. Provide the buyer with an EPA pamphlet titled *Protect Your Family From Lead In Your Home*

c. Offer the prospective buyer 5 days to inspect for lead-based paint and lead-based paint hazards

d. Offer the prospective buyer 3 days to inspect for lead-based paint and lead-based paint hazards

50. Categories of stigmatized properties include

a. Properties that were once used as brothels

b. Properties located in floodplains

c. Properties with defective heaters

d. Properties with leaky roofs

51. A seller of a single-family home tells the listing agent that she is moving because of gang activity nearby. The agent should

a. Contact the police

b. Keep the seller's information confidential because the agent's fiduciary duty to the seller includes loyalty and confidentiality

c. Disclose this fact to potential purchasers

d. Only schedule showings after sunset

52. Sandra is a Florida real estate broker who received conflicting demands for trust funds from the buyer and seller of a shopping center. In conformity with Florida law, Sandra notified the FREC of the conflicting demands of the buyer and seller on the 10th business day after the last party's demand. Assuming that the matter does not settle in the meanwhile, Sandra must institute one of the approved a settlement procedures as set forth in Florida Statutes within how many business days of her notification to the FREC of the conflicting demands?

a. 30

b. 20

c. 15

d. 10

53. If I promise to pay you $20 if you mow my lawn on Tuesday, and you shrug your shoulders and say, "I'll see if I have time," we have

a. An express, bilateral contract

b. An implied, unilateral contract

c. An express, unilateral contract

d. An implied, bilateral contract

54. The consent of the parties to a contract must be

a. Mutual, communicated by each to the other, in writing

b. Freely given, in writing, mutual

c. Freely given, in writing, communicated by each to the other

d. Freely given, mutual, communicated by each to the other

55. A provision in a contract that specifies exactly the amount of damages to be paid by the breaching party for a breach is called a

a. Safety clause

b. Contingency clause

c. Liquidated damages clause

d. Severability clause

56. Emily is a Florida real estate broker who, during negotiations for the purchase of a home, refers the potential buyer to ABC Carpets.

a. Emily may receive a referral fee from ABC Carpets without informing either the seller or the potential buyer regardless of the amount of the referral fee.

b. Emily may receive a referral fee from ABC Carpets without informing either the seller or the potential buyer as long as the referral fee does not exceed $50.

c. Emily may receive a referral fee from ABC Carpets without informing either the seller or the potential buyer as long as the referral fee does not exceed $75.

d. Emily may not receive a referral fee from ABC Carpets without informing the seller and the potential buyer of all facts pertaining to the referral fee.

57. A lease transfers an estate in the real property leased. This transfer of a real property interest creates between the landlord and the tenant

a. Privity of estate

b. Privity of contract

c. Chattel real

d. Profit á prendre

58. Randy owns a shoe store in a shopping mall. His lease calls for a base rent amount plus 1% of the gross receipts of his store. What type of lease does Randy have?

a. Net lease

b. Graduated lease

c. Percentage lease

d. Ground lease

59. An owner of an apartment complex

a. May pay a finder's fee or referral fee to an unlicensed person who is a tenant in such apartment complex provided the value of the fee does not exceed $25 per transaction and provided that the referral is for the rental or lease of a unit in the apartment complex.

b. May pay a finder's fee or referral fee to an unlicensed person who is a tenant in such apartment complex provided the value of the fee does not exceed $50 per transaction and provided that the referral is for the rental or lease of a unit in the apartment complex.

c. May pay a finder's fee or referral fee to an unlicensed person who is a tenant in such apartment complex provided the value of the fee does not exceed $75 per transaction and provided that the referral is for the rental or lease of a unit in the apartment complex.

d. May not pay a finder's fee or referral fee to any unlicensed person, regardless as to whether that unlicensed person is a tenant of the apartment complex, for a referral for the rental or lease of a unit in the apartment complex.

60. An offer and acceptance of a contract refers to

a. The execution of the contract

b. The object of the contract

c. A meeting of the minds

d. The consideration of the contract

61. Emily signed a purchase agreement with John that states that if John breaches the agreement and fails to close the transaction, then Emily will accept John's earnest money deposit as the only damages John would have to pay. Under their agreement, John's forfeiting of his earnest money deposit would represent

a. Specific performance

b. Compensatory damages

c. Liquidated damages

d. Rescission

62. A net listing cannot be

a. An exclusive agency listing

b. An open listing

c. An exclusive right to sell listing

d. None of the above

63. John's contract with Joe states that if any term of the contract is held to be ineffective or invalid, the remaining contract terms should nevertheless be given full force and effect. This contract term is called a

a. Severability clause

b. Safety clause

c. Revocation clause

d. Ironclad merger clause

64. Evaluate the following two statements: (1) consideration for a contract need not be monetary; (2) the statute of limitations requires that certain contracts must be in writing to be enforceable.

a. Both statements are correct.

b. The first statement is correct and the second statement is false.

c. The first statement is false and the second statement is true.

d. Both statements are false.

65. Which of the following statements is false?

a. A lease-option provides that the lessee has the right to purchase the property at the specified price and terms any time prior to a specified date, but has no obligation to do so.

b. A graduated lease is similar to a gross lease except that it provides for periodic increases in the rent, often based on the Consumer Price Index.

c. In an option contract, the optionee grants to the optionor the right to purchase property for a specific sum at any time during the option term without creating an obligation by the optionee to do so.

d. Under a gross lease, the tenant pays a fixed rental amount, and the landlord pays all of the operating expenses for the premises.

66. Which, if any, of the following types of business entities may not register as a Florida real estate broker?

a. Corporations

b. Limited liability companies

c. Limited liability partnerships

d. Each of the above may register as a Florida real estate broker.

67. Typically, a lender's title insurance policy

a. Protects the borrower up to the amount of principal outstanding on the loan

b. Protects the borrower up to the purchase price of the property

c. Protects the lender up to the purchase price of the property

d. Protects the lender up to the amount of principal outstanding on the loan

68. A chain of title is

a. A complete chronological history of all documents affecting the title to a property

b. A statement by the title insurance company of the condition of the title and of the terms and conditions upon which it is willing to issue a policy

c. A duplicate of county title records maintained at title insurance companies for use in title searches

d. A court proceeding intended to establish the true ownership of a property

69. A general warranty deed conveys a warranty that the grantor's are the owners of the property and have the right to convey it. This type of warranty is referred to as what type of covenant?

a. Quiet enjoyment

b. Seisin

c. Against encumbrances

d. Further assurance

70. Which of the following business entities may register as a Florida real estate broker?

a. Business trusts

b. Cooperative associations

c. Limited liability partnerships

d. Unincorporated associations

71. Rent is typically paid in _____, in which case the seller would be _____ for the portion of the month remaining after closing.

a. Advance, credited

b. Advance, debited

c. Arrears, credited

d. Arrears, debited

72. Under Florida real estate law, an unlicensed personal assistant of a sales associate may perform which of the following activities on behalf of the sales associate?

a. Assemble documents for closing.

b. Negotiate the rent for a single-family home.

c. Auction a parcel of real property.

d. None of the above.

73. Homeowners of personal residences are eligible for certain federal income tax benefits, which do not include

a. A certain amount of interest paid on a mortgage secured by a principal residence or by a second home

b. Property taxes paid on the homeowner's residence

c. Private mortgage insurance premiums

d. Mortgage loan prepayment penalties

74. A final order has been issued by the FREC suspending the license of a sales associate. If the sales associate wishes to appeal this final order the sales associate must file a notice of appeal within how many days of the rendering of the final order?

a. 10

b. 15

c. 30

d. 45

75. A passive investor is someone

a. Who actively participates in the activities of a business not invested in.

b. Who does not actively participate in the activities of a business invested in.

c. Who does not actively participate in the activities of a business not invested in.

d. Who actively participates in the activities of the business invested in.

76. A restructuring of a mortgage or deed of trust on terms more favorable to the borrower's ability to continue making loan payments is a

a. Short sale

b. Deed in lieu of foreclosure

c. Loan modification

d. Loan alternative

77. A person is not qualified to make a claim for recovery from the Real Estate Recovery Fund, if

a. The person is the spouse of the judgment debtor

b. The judgment is against a real estate brokerage corporation, partnership, limited liability company, or limited liability partnership

c. The person's claim is based upon a real estate transaction in which the broker or sales associate did not hold a valid, current, and active license at the time of the real estate transaction

d. Any of the above

78. If, after _____, it is found that the account balance is less than it should be, there is a _____.

a. Reconciliation, trust fund shortage

b. Reconciliation, conversion

c. Commingling, conversion

d. Reconciliation, trust fund overage

79. The Federal Fair Housing Act does not prohibit

a. Refusal to loan in particular areas

b. Representing that prices will decline, or crime increase, or other negative effects will occur because of the entrance of minorities into particular areas

c. Conduct against a person because such person has been convicted of the illegal manufacture or distribution of a controlled substance

d. Discriminatory access to multiple listing services

80. A for-profit private club owns a building in which there are 5 hotel-type guestrooms, a meeting hall, a recreation room, a dining room, and other amenities used by guests. This club has a policy of only renting their guestrooms to members of the club. Under the Federal Fair Housing Act this policy is

a. Legal because private clubs are exempt under the FFHA

b. Illegal because no private club is exempt under the FFHA

c. Legal because the federal government does not restrict the activities of private clubs

d. Illegal because for-profit private clubs are not exempt under the FFHA.

81. The Americans with Disabilities Act does not

a. Provide for monetary damages

b. Allow private individuals to receive back pay

c. Allow private individuals to receive injunctive relief for violations of its employment requirements

d. Allow private individuals to receive injunctive relief for violations of its public accommodation requirements

82. A Florida real estate licensee whose actions resulted in payment to a claimant from the Real Estate Recovery Fund

a. May, at the discretion of the FREC, automatically result in the suspension licensee's license

b. Automatically has his or her license suspended

c. Automatically has his or her license suspended, which license shall be reinstated upon payment in full of the amount paid from the Fund.

d. May, at the discretion of the DRE, automatically result in the suspension of the licensee's license

83. A broker publishes an advertisement for a home in which the following words appear: "Just two blocks from a popular Jewish deli." This ad probably is

a. Legal because it is entirely accurate

b. Legal because it is entirely accurate, and the broker is Jewish

c. Legal because it is entirely accurate, and the broker is of Korean descent

d. Illegal

84. When a tenant vacates the premises at the termination of the lease, if the landlord intends to impose a claim on the tenant's security deposit, the landlord must, within how many days, give the tenant written notice by certified mail to the tenant's last known mailing address of the landlord's intention to impose a claim on the deposit and the reason for imposing the claim?

a. 45

b. 30

c. 15

d. 10

85. For an apartment building, which of the following is not subject to a federal tax depreciation deduction?

a. The cost of the structure

b. The cost of the swimming pool

c. The cost of the land on which the structure was built

d. The cost of the recreation room

86. A a subdivider will prepare a ____, which is a detailed map showing the boundaries of the individual parcels, streets, easements, engineering data, and, often, the environmental impact of the development.

a. Lot

b. Tract

c. Block

d. Plat

87. In Florida, a year-to-year tenancy may be terminated by either party

a. By giving not less than 180 days' notice prior to the end of any annual period

b. By giving not less than 90 days' notice prior to the end of any annual period

c. By giving not less than 60 days' notice prior to the end of any annual period

d. By giving not less than 30 days' notice prior to the end of any annual period

88. Which of the following statements is true?

a. It is not an antitrust violation for a broker acting alone to refuse to do business except in specific areas.

b. It is an antitrust violation for a broker acting alone to refuse to do business with another broker.

c. Under the Sherman Act, the term "group action" refers to three or more persons agreeing to act.

d. It is not an antitrust violation for two competing brokers to agree not to do business with a broker whom they believe to be dishonest.

89. Susan is a land developer, and Emily is a broker whom Susan approaches to handle the sale of one of Susan's newly developed lots. Emily agrees to handle the sale, but only on condition that Susan agrees to hire Emily to sell Susan's remaining lots. This is an example of

a. A tying arrangement

b. Market allocation

c. Price-fixing

d. Group boycott

90. If a loan has an LTV of 85%, an appraised value of $210,000, and a sales price of $215,000, what is the amount of the loan if the LTV was based on the lesser of the appraised value or the sales price?

a. $182,750

b. $210,000

c. $215,000

d. None of the above

91. John and Margaret are a married couple who reside on Florida property they own that lies outside of any municipality. Under Florida homestead law, John and Margaret may declare a homestead consisting of

a. Up to 160 acres of contiguous land, upon which the exemption shall be limited to the land and the residence of the owner or the owner's family

b. Up to 100 acres of contiguous land, upon which the exemption shall be limited to the land and the residence of the owner or the owner's family

c. Up to 160 acres of contiguous land and all improvements thereon

d. Up to 100 acres of contiguous land and all improvements thereon

92. Under Florida's adverse possession law, which, if any, of the following statements is false?

a. To acquire adverse possession of a property, a person must have had continual possession of the property for at least 7 years.

b. To acquire adverse possession of a property, a person must have paid all outstanding taxes on the property within one year of entering into possession.

c. To acquire adverse possession of a property, the possession must have been under claim of title.

d. All of the above statements are false.

93. Harvey's home is appraised at $250,000. The first mortgage against his home has an outstanding balance of $150,000. Harvey has just arranged to obtain a home equity line of credit in the amount of 80% of the appraised value of his home, minus the total outstanding indebtedness against the home. What is the amount of his line of credit?

a. $80,000

b. $50,000

c. $200,000

d. $120,000

94. Pursuant to Florida's statute of frauds, each of the following agreements or promises is unenforceable unless the agreement or promise, or some note or memorandum thereof, is in writing and signed by the party, or by an authorized agent of the party, to be charged, except

a. A lease for a period of one year

b. An agreement that is not to be performed within the space of 1 year of its signing

c. An agreement for the sale of real estate

d. All of the choices a-c are unenforceable under Florida's statute of frauds.

71

95. Kathy is a salesperson who receives 45% of the total commission received by her broker from the sale of a house Kathy listed. What is the broker's net share of the commission if the house sold for $845,000, the commission rate was 6%, and a cooperating broker received half of the commission?

a. $11,407.50

b. $13,942.50

c. $27,885.00

d. None of the above

96. Which, if any, of the following statements is (are) true?

a. Florida real estate licensees must give the principal(s) a legible, signed, true and correct copy of the listing agreement within 48 hours of obtaining the written listing agreement.

b. A written listing agreement may not contain an automatic renewal clause.

c. Both a and b.

d. Neither a nor b.

97. Which of the following statements regarding Florida's documentary stamp tax on notes is true?

a. The tax rate is 35 cents on each $100 or fraction thereof of the indebtedness or obligation evidenced in the notes.

b. The tax on any note may not exceed $2,450.

c. Both a and b

d. Neither a nor b

98. You pass out while shopping. Someone calls 9/11, the paramedics come, and an ambulance takes you (still unconscious) to the nearest emergency room. A month later you get a bill from the ambulance company in an amount that is the going rate in your city.

a. You do not have to pay the bill because there was no mutual consent — no "meeting of the minds."

b. You do not have to pay the bill because you never made a promise to do so.

c. You do not have to pay because you were not informed of the cost and never agreed to pay it.

d. You owe the ambulance company the amount of their bill.

99. Amelia purchased a Florida condo for $125,000, paying $25,000 cash, assuming the seller's outstanding mortgage of $37,000, and taking out a new mortgage in the amount of $63,000. The Florida intangible tax on all notes, bonds, and other obligations for payment of money that are secured by mortgages would be

a. $126

b. $200

c. $250

d. $350

100. In Florida, any change resulting from reassessment of homesteaded property may not exceed

a. 3% of the assessed value of the property for the prior year or the percentage change in the consumer price index for the preceding calendar year, whichever is greater

b. 3% of the assessed value of the property for the prior year or the percentage change in the consumer price index for the preceding calendar year, whichever is lower

c. 5% of the assessed value of the property for the prior year or the percentage change in the consumer price index for the preceding calendar year, whichever is greater

d. 5% of the assessed value of the property for the prior year or the percentage change in the consumer price index for the preceding calendar year, whichever is lower

ANSWERS TO PRACTICE EXAM #1:

Abbreviations used in this Practice Exam are:

DBPR — Department of Business and Professional Regulation
FAC — Florida Administrative Code
FREC — Florida Real Estate Commission
FS — Florida Statutes

1. **c.** FS, 475.17(3)(c), states that the "license of any sales associate who does not complete the postlicensure education requirement prior to the first renewal following initial licensure shall be considered null and void. Such person wishing to again operate as a real estate sales associate must requalify by satisfactorily completing the sales associate's prelicensure course and passing the state examination for licensure as a sales associate."

2. **a.** Trade fixtures are personal property. Each of the other choices are examples of real property.

3. **c.** A salary is considered compensation, and there is no exemption in FS, 475, for an employee of a brokerage office who performs real estate services. Exemptions for persons identified in a, b, and d can be found in FS, 475.011.

4. **b.** The metes and bounds system starts at a point of beginning, then works around the parcel, and finally ends at the beginning point.

5. **d.** FS, 177.031(14), states that the term "plat" refers to "a map or delineated representation of the subdivision of lands, being a complete exact representation of the subdivision and other information in compliance with the requirement of all applicable sections of this part and of any local ordinances."

6. **d.** (the lesser of the appraised value or $275,000) $\times$ .8 = $220,000.
(the lesser of the appraised value or $275,000) = $220,000 $\div$ .8 = $275,000.
Therefore, the appraised value of the home is $275,000 or greater.

7. **b.** Real estate taxes, special assessments, and subordination agreements present exceptions to the general lien priority of first to record, first in right.

8. **d.** An easement in gross is an easement that benefits a legal person rather than other land.

9. **c.** FS, 475.23, provides that a "license shall cease to be in force whenever a broker changes her or his business address, a real estate school operating under a permit issued pursuant to s. 475.451 changes its business address, or a sales associate working for a broker or an instructor working for a real estate school changes employer. The licensee shall notify the commission of the change no later than 10 days after the change, on a form provided by the commission."

10. **a.** A corporation may not be a joint tenant because the law regards a corporation as having potentially infinite duration, and infinite duration would result in the right of survivorship having no consequence.

11. **d.** A fixture is a thing that starts out as personal property but then is attached to the land in such a manner as to be considered real property.

12. **a.** FS, 475.215, provides that a "licensed broker may be issued upon request additional licenses as a broker, but not as a sales associate or as a broker associate, whenever it is clearly shown that the requested additional licenses are necessary to the conduct of real estate brokerage business and that the additional licenses will not be used in a manner likely to be prejudicial or harmful to any person, including a licensee under this chapter."

13.   **a.** Eminent domain is a right of the state to take, through due process proceedings (often referred to as condemnation proceedings), private property for public use upon payment of just compensation.

14.   **c.** The primary purpose of escheat is to prevent property from remaining ownerless or abandoned.

15.   **b.** Conditional use refers to an exception for special uses such as churches, schools, and hospitals that wish to locate to areas zoned exclusively for residential use.

16.   **b.** FS, 475.278(1)(b), states that it will be "presumed that all licensees are operating as transaction brokers unless a single agent or no brokerage relationship is established, in writing, with a customer."

17.   **a.** Removal actions are usually short-term responses to a perceived imminent threat that requires a prompt response.

18.   **a.** Covenants, conditions, and restrictions (CC&Rs) generally are negative covenants whereby persons agree to limit certain things, such as the color of paint on houses or the type of architecture used to build or remodel houses.

19.   **a.** Because Bob clearly violated a condition in the deed restriction, Arnold may bring an action to enforce the condition through forfeiture of title.

20.   **b.** FS, 475.274, states that a written brokerage relationship disclosure must be made only when dealing with residential real estate transactions, therefore, choice c is incorrect. FS, 475.278(4) requires that no brokerage relationships must be disclosed in writing when dealing with residential real estate transactions. Finally, there is no requirement that a transactional brokerage relationship must be disclosed in writing unless a single agency relationship is being changed to a transaction brokerage relationship, in which case a written consent of the principal must be obtained. FS, 278(3)(b)2.

21.   **a.** Nonconforming use refers to an exception for areas that are zoned for the first time or that are rezoned and where established property uses that previously were permitted do not conform to the new zoning requirements. As a general rule, such existing properties are "grandfathered in," allowing them to continue the old use but not to extend the old use to additional properties or to continue the old use after rebuilding or abandonment.

22.   **b.** Market price is the price actually paid for a particular property.

23.   **b.** The principle of regression states that the value of a residence of higher value tends to be degraded by the proximity to residences of lower value.

24.   **c.** The income approach determines the market value of the subject property by capitalizing the estimated future income of the property.

25.   **d.** Choice a is false because Jonathan owes fiduciary duties to the seller not to the buyer. Choice b is false because, pursuant to FS, 275.2755(1), in a designated sales associate situation, the buyer and seller must *each* have assets of $1 million or more. Choice c is false because Florida real estate law permits designated sales associate relationships under certain conditions, as specified in FS, 275.2755(1).

26.   **a.** If a feature of a comparable is inferior to the same type of feature in the subject property, then the difference in value of features is added to the comparable property.

27.   **a.** FS, 475.278(4)a, provides that "a real estate licensee owes to a potential seller or buyer with whom the licensee has no brokerage relationship the following duties: 1.

Dealing honestly and fairly; 2. Disclosing all known facts that materially affect the value of the residential real property which are not readily observable to the buyer; and 3. Accounting for all funds entrusted to the licensee.

28. **c.** For appraisal purposes, depreciation is defined as the loss in value due to any cause.

29. **a.** The return on investment of a property is calculated by dividing the investor's cash flow (net income minus financing charges) by the investor's actual cash investment.

30. **d.** A significant risk of leveraging is that if property values fall, rental values will fall, possibly resulting in negative cash flow to the leveraged investor.

31. **d.** FS, 475.22(1), provides that each "active broker shall maintain an office, which shall consist of at least *one* enclosed room in a building of stationary construction." (emphasis added). Choice a is correct pursuant to FAC, 61J2-10.025(3)(a). Choice b is correct pursuant to FAC, 61J2-10.022. Choice is correct pursuant to FAC, 61J2-10.025(2).

32. **c.** A preliminary title report does not include an appraisal of the property.

33. **b.** In an adjustable-rate mortgage, the fully indexed rate is equal to the index plus the margin.

34. **c.** A reverse mortgage is a loan for homeowners 62 years of age or older who have a large amount of equity in their homes, usually designed to provide such homeowners with monthly payments, often over the lifetime of the last surviving homeowner who either moves out of the house or dies.

35. **b.** One of the disadvantages of FHA-insured loans is the relatively low loan amount insured.

36. **b.** FAC, 61J2-14.009 provides that every "sales associate who receives any deposit … shall deliver the same to the broker or employer no later than the end of the next business day following receipt of the item to be deposited. Saturday, Sundays and legal holidays shall not be construed as business days."

37. **b.** A defeasance clause states that that when the loan debt has been fully paid, the lender must release the property from the lien so that legal title free from the lien will be owned by the borrower.

38. **c.** An agent for a particular act or transaction is a special agent.

39. **b.** FAC, 61J2-14.010, states that every broker receives from a sales associate a good-faith deposit must "immediately" deposit the good-faith deposit. FAC, 61J2-14.008(3), provides that the word "immediately" means "the placement of a deposit in an escrow account no later than the end of the third business day following receipt of the item to be deposited." FAC, 61J2-14.009, provides that receipt "by a sales associate or any other representative of the brokerage firm constitutes receipt by the broker." *Therefore, even though Kathy did not have the good-faith deposit in hand until Friday, she nevertheless was in "receipt" of the good-faith deposit on Thursday, pursuant to FAC, 61J2-14.009.* Therefore, Friday counts as day one, Monday as day two, and Tuesday as day three.

40. **a.** Ostensible agency is created when a principal intentionally, or by want of ordinary care, causes a third person to believe another to be his agent who is not actually employed by the principal.

41. **a.** There is a rule of equity known as estoppel that holds that one who causes another to rely on his or her words or actions shall be prohibited from later taking a contrary position detrimental to the person who so relied.

42. **b.** A subagent is an agent of an agent.

43. **d.** FAC, 61J2-14.014 (1), provides that a "broker is allowed to place escrow funds in an interest-bearing account. The placement of escrow monies in an interest-bearing account, designation of the party who is to receive the interest, and the time the earned interest must be disbursed, must be done with the written permission of all the parties to the transaction. Said escrow account must be in an insured account in a depository located and doing business in Florida."

44. **b.** Placing funds belonging to clients or customers into accounts also holding the agent's funds is considered commingling.

45. **c.** Termination of agency by force of law can occur for several reasons, including bankruptcy, change in law, or loss of license.

46. **a.** If a broker supplies financing to build a house with the stipulation that the broker will have the listing to sell the house, the broker's agency is coupled with an interest, which has the legal effect of making the appointment of the broker irrevocable.

47. **b.** FS, 475.5015, provides that each "broker shall preserve at least one legible copy of all books, accounts, and records pertaining to her or his real estate brokerage business for at least 5 years from the date of receipt of any money, fund, deposit, check, or draft entrusted to the broker or, in the event no funds are entrusted to the broker, for at least 5 years from the date of execution by any party of any listing agreement, offer to purchase, rental property management agreement, rental or lease agreement, or any other written or verbal agreement which engages the services of the broker."

48. **c.** Amanda's fiduciary duty to the seller prevents her from telling a prospective buyer that the seller is willing to take a lower price unless the seller gives Amanda permission to do so.

49. **b.** The seller of a residential dwelling unit built before 1978 must provide the buyer with an EPA pamphlet titled *Protect Your Family From Lead In Your Home*.

50. **a.** A stigmatized property is a property having a condition that certain persons may find materially negative in a way that does not relate to the property's actual physical condition.

51. **c.** Known external conditions that, because of their severity, may rise to the level of material facts (such as neighbors who throw loud parties, neighbors with dogs that bark throughout the night, gang activity nearby, etc.) should be disclosed.

52. **b.** FAC, 61J2-10.032(1)(a), provides that a "real estate broker, upon receiving conflicting demands for any trust funds being maintained in the broker's escrow account, must provide written notification to the Commission within 15 business days of the last party's demand and the broker must institute one of the settlement procedures as set forth in Section 475.25(1)(d)1., Florida Statutes, *within 30 business days after the last demand*." (emphasis added) Because Sandra notified the commission on the 10th business day after receiving the last party's demand, she has 20 more business days in which institute one of the approved settlement procedures as set forth in Florida Statutes.

53. **c.** The contract between us is express (my promise was verbal), and it is unilateral because only I have made a promise to pay you upon the happening of a contingency.

54. **d.** The consent of the parties to a contract must be freely given, mutual, and communicated by each to the other.

55. **c.** A liquidated damages clause is a provision in a contract that specifies exactly the amount of damages to be paid by the breaching party for a breach.

56. **d.** FAC, 61J2-10.028(1), provides that a real estate licensee may not receive any kickback or rebate for referring a client or customer to any business related to any transaction negotiated or handled by the licensee, unless prior to the time of the referral the licensee fully advises all affected parties in the transaction of all facts pertaining to the arrangement of kickbacks or rebates.

57. **a.** A lease transfers an estate in the real property leased. This transfer of a real property creates privity of estate between the landlord and the tenant.

58. **c.** Under a percentage lease, which is often used in shopping centers, the tenant typically pays a base rent amount plus a percentage of the gross receipts of the tenant's business.

59. **b.** FS, 475.001(13), provides that a property management firm or an owner of an apartment complex may pay a finder's fee or referral fee to an unlicensed person *who is a tenant in such apartment complex* provided the value of the fee does not exceed $50 per transaction and provided that the referral is for the rental or lease of a unit in the apartment complex. FS, 475.001(13), further provides that it is a violation for a property management firm or an owner of apartment complex to pay a finder's fee to an unlicensed person who is not a tenant of the apartment complex.

60. **c.** A meeting of the minds is usually evidenced by an offer by one party that manifests contractual intention and an acceptance by the other party.

61. **c.** Parties may agree, usually in a building contract, or in a contract to purchase real estate, that if a breach occurs, a specified amount of damages, referred to as liquidated damages, will be paid in lieu of any other remedy for the breach.

62. **d.** A net listing can take the form of any of the three basic types of listings.

63. **a.** A severability clause is a contract provision providing that if any term of the agreement is held to be ineffective or invalid, the remaining provisions will nevertheless be given full force and effect.

64. **b.** Consideration need not be monetary; it can, for example, be a forbearance. The second statement refers to the statute of frauds, not the statute of limitations.

65. **c.** In an option contract, the *optionor* grants to the *optionee* the right to purchase property for a specific sum at any time during the option term without creating an obligation by the optionee to do so.

66. **d.** FS, 475.15, provides that each "partnership, limited liability partnership, limited liability company, or corporation which acts as a broker shall register with the commission and shall renew the licenses or registrations of its members, officers, and directors for each license period."

67. **d.** In most real estate transactions, the lender requires that the buyer pay for a lender's policy of title insurance that protects the lender up to the amount of principal outstanding on the loan.

68. **a.** A chain of title is a complete chronological history of all documents affecting the title to a property.

69. **b.** A covenant of seisin is a warranty by the grantor's that they are the owners of the property and have the right to convey it.

70. **c.** FS, 475.15, provides that each "partnership, limited liability partnership, limited liability company, or corporation which acts as a broker shall register with the commission and shall renew the licenses or registrations of its members, officers, and directors for each license period." There is no provision for allowing business trusts, cooperative associations, or unincorporated associations to be registered as real estate brokers.

71. **b.** Rent is typically paid in advance, in which case the seller would be debited for the portion of the month remaining after closing.

72. **a.** FS, 475.01(1)(a), presents a list of activities brokers and sales associates may perform that require real estate licenses. Among of those activities are the negotiating of rents and conducting auctions of real property. Choice a is among the activities that unlicensed personal assistants may perform pursuant to the guideline "Permissible Activities of an Unlicensed Assistant" approved by the FREC, which, at the time of this writing, can be found at www.myfloridalicense.com/dbpr/re/documents/Permissibleactivitiesrev092009.pdf.

73. **c.** Private mortgage insurance premiums are not a tax-deductible expense for owners of homes that are not income producing properties.

74. **c.** FS, 120.68(2)(a), provides that such an appeal must be filed within 30 days of the rendering of the final order.

75. **b.** An active investor is someone who actively participates in the activities of a business invested in (for example, an individual who manages his or her own rental properties), as distinguished from a passive investor, who is someone who does not actively participate in the activities of a business invested in.

76. **c.** Loan modification is a restructuring or modification of a mortgage or deed of trust on terms more favorable to the borrower's ability (or desire) to continue making loan payments.

77. **d.** FS, 475.483(2)(2), provides that a person is not qualified to make a claim for recovery from the Real Estate Recovery Fund in various circumstances, including those listed in choices a-c.

78. **a.** If, after reconciliation, it is found that the account balance is less than it should be, there is a trust fund shortage.

79. **c.** The Federal Fair Housing Act does not prohibit conduct against a person because such person has been convicted of the illegal manufacture or distribution of a controlled substance.

80. **d.** The FFHA exemption for private clubs only applies to nonprofit private clubs.

81. **a.** The ADA allows private individuals to receive back pay and injunctive relief for violations of its employment requirements and injunctive relief for violation of its public accommodation requirements, but does not provide for monetary damages.

82. **b.** FS, 475.484(7), provides that upon "the payment of any amount from the Real Estate Recovery Fund in settlement of a claim in satisfaction of a judgment against a broker or sales associate... the license of such broker or sales associate shall be automatically suspended upon the date of payment from the fund. The license of such broker or sales associate may not be reinstated until the licensee has repaid in full, *plus interest*, the amount paid from the fund." Note that the clause "plus interest" makes choice c incorrect. Furthermore, FS, 475.484(7), does not state that the license "shall be reinstated..." It merely states that the license "may not be reinstated until..."

83. **d.** Accuracy is not a defense to HUD's rules on advertising for housing, which prohibit advertising that conveys either overt or tacit discriminatory preferences or limitations.

84.   **b.** FS, 83.49(3)(a), provides that upon "the vacating of the premises for termination of the lease, if the landlord does not intend to impose a claim on the security deposit, the landlord shall have 15 days to return the security deposit together with interest if otherwise required, or the landlord shall have 30 days to give the tenant written notice by certified mail to the tenant's last known mailing address of his or her intention to impose a claim on the deposit and the reason for imposing the claim."

85.   **c.** Only the cost of improvements is subject to a depreciation deduction; the cost of land is not.

86.   **d.** A subdivider must draw up plans to comply with all of the many subdivision regulations applicable to the land the subdivider intends to develop. The subdivider will prepare a plat, which is a detailed map showing the boundaries of the individual parcels, streets, easements, engineering data, and, often, the environmental impact of the development.

87.   **c.** FS, 83.57(1), provides that a year-to-year tenancy may be terminated by either party "by giving not less than 60 days' notice prior to the end of any annual period."

88.   **a.** An antitrust violation for market allocation requires two or more competitors to agree to act. Therefore a broker acting alone would not violate antitrust law, though such actions may violate other laws, such as fair housing laws, if the broker is in fact discriminating against a protected class.

89.   **a.** In real estate agency, a typical case of an *impermissible* tying arrangement occurs when the sale of a property is conditioned upon the agent's obtaining the listing for future sales.

90.   **d.** Here, LTV = .85 = (amount of the loan) ÷ $210,000. Therefore, the amount of the loan is $210,000 × .85 = $178,500.

91.   **c.** Article X, Section 4, of the Florida Constitution states that a homestead, if located outside a municipality, shall consist of up to the extent of one hundred sixty acres of contiguous land and improvements thereon.

92.   **d.** FS, 95.18(1), lists conditions for acquiring property by adverse possession, which conditions include those in choices a-c. Therefore, the only choice that is false is choice d.

93.   **b.** ($250,000 × .8) - $150,000 = $50,000.

94.   **a.** FS, 725.01, provides a list of agreements and promises that are unenforceable, including choices b and c. Regarding choice a, FS, 725.01, provides that a lease for a period *longer than one year* is unenforceable unless the lease, or some note or memorandum thereof, is in writing and signed by the party, or by an authorized agent of the party, to be charged.

95.   **b.** Kathy's broker's gross is 3% of the sales price of $845,000, which is .03 × $845,000 = $25,350. The broker's rent is 55% of $25,350 = $13,942.50.

96.   **b.** FS, 475.25(1)(r), provides that a licensee must "give the principal(s) a legible, signed, true and correct copy of the listing agreement within 24 hours of obtaining the written listing agreement. The written listing agreement shall contain no provision requiring the person signing the listing to notify the broker of the intention to cancel the listing after such definite expiration date." The last sentence implies that a written listing agreement may not contain an automatic renewal clause.

97.   **c.** FS, 201.08, provides that the stamp tax on notes "shall be 35 cents on each $100 or fraction thereof of the indebtedness or obligation evidenced thereby. The tax on any document described in this paragraph may not exceed $2,450."

98.   **d.** There was an implied contract created here. All terms of a contract can be implied, depending on the circumstances.

99.   **a.** FS, 199.133, and FS, 199.145 provide for an intangible tax of 2 mils per dollar only on new mortgages, *not on mortgages that are assumed.* Therefore, the Florida intangible tax related to this transaction would be $0.002 \times 63,000 = $126.

100.   **b.** Pursuant to FS 193.155(1), any "change resulting from such reassessment shall not exceed the lower of the following: (a) Three percent of the assessed value of the property for the prior year; or (b) The percentage change in the Consumer Price Index for All Urban Consumers, U.S. City Average, all items 1967=100, or successor reports for the preceding calendar year as initially reported by the United States Department of Labor, Bureau of Labor Statistics."

PRACTICE EXAM #2:

Abbreviations used in this Practice Exam are:

DBPR — Department of Business and Professional Regulation
FAC — Florida Administrative Code
FREC — Florida Real Estate Commission
FS — Florida Statutes

1. The FREC may discipline a real estate licensee who fails, within how many days, to notify the DBPR of the licensee being convicted or found guilty of, or of entering a plea of nolo contendere or guilty to, a crime in any jurisdiction?

a. 15

b. 30

c. 45

d. 60

2. A description such as T2N, R3E, SBL&M would be what kind of land description?

a. U.S. government survey system

b. Metes and bounds system

c. Lot, block, and tract system

d. Recorded plat system

3. As defined in Florida Statutes, Chapter 475, the term "residential sale" includes the sale of

a. Residential property of five or fewer units

b. The sale of unimproved residential property intended for use of five or fewer units

c. The sale of agricultural property of 10 or fewer acres

d. None of the above

4. The key to the front door of a house would most likely be characterized as

a. Personal property

b. An emblement

c. Real property

d. An easement

5. There are many members of the Florida Real Estate Commission (FREC)?

a. 3

b. 5

c. 7

d. 9

6. Federal tax liens are _____ and _____ liens.

a. Specific, involuntary

b. General, involuntary

c. Specific, voluntary

d. General, voluntary

7. The most important feature distinguishing a joint tenancy from a tenancy in common is

a. Percentage of ownership

b. The ability to transfer the tenants' interests

c. The percentage of possession

d. The right of survivorship

8. Which of the following statements is false about a tenancy in common?

a. All of the tenants have an undivided interest in the property.

b. The tenants may not transfer their interests by will.

c. The tenancy may be terminated by a voluntary partition.

d. Each tenant may sell his or her interest in the tenancy.

9. If a sales associate or broker associate changes employers, the Florida Real Estate Commission must be notified within how many days of the change?

a. 7

b. 10

c. 14

d. 20

10. One of the advantages of condominium ownership over single-family-home ownership is

a. No maintenance

b. No homeowners association

c. Deductibility of mortgage interest

d. Ease of maintenance

11. An object that a tenant attaches to real property for use in the tenant's trade or business is

a. An easement appurtenant

b. A trade fixture

c. An easement in gross

d. An encroachment

12. If a Florida real estate licensee is a member of the Armed Forces of the United States, is on active duty, and is not engaged in activities requiring a real estate license in the private sector for profit, such real estate licensee is required to renew his or her license

a. Within one year of discharge from active duty

b. Within six months of discharge from active duty

c. Immediately upon discharge from active duty

d. Every two years

13. To exercise eminent domain, an appropriate governmental body must satisfy certain requirements, including

a. That the property must be taken for the public good

b. That the governmental body must pay at least 110% of the property's assessed value

c. That the governmental body demonstrate that the taking will result in an increase in the property's fair market value

d. That the governmental body must demonstrate that the property was not used in conformance with existing zoning laws

14. Properties that are granted a nonconforming use exception are said to be

a. Spot zoned

b. At variance

c. Buffered in

d. Grandfathered in

15. Brownfields are defined by the EPA as

a. Real property, the expansion, redevelopment, or reuse of which may be complicated by the presence or potential presence of a hazardous substance, pollutant, or contaminant.

b. Areas that are soaked or flooded by surface or groundwater frequently enough or for sufficient duration to support plants, birds, animals, and aquatic life. Wetlands generally include swamps, marshes, bugs, estuaries, and other inland and coastal areas, and are federally protected

c. Areas of low, flat, periodically flooded land near streams or rivers

d. A large hole used for the purpose of waste disposal

16. A Florida real estate transaction broker owes each of the following duties to each of his or her customers, except

a. Dealing with each customer honestly and fairly

b. Representing each customer with skill, care, and diligence

c. Presenting all offers and counteroffers in a timely manner, unless a party has previously directed the licensee otherwise in writing

d. Representing each customer as a fiduciary

17. A known cause of cancers in animals and possibly in humans that is extensively used to make building materials is

a. Radon

b. Mesothelioma

c. Formaldehyde

d. Carbon monoxide

18. A local government will implement a master plan through all of the following except

a. Setback restrictions

b. Taxation

c. Inverse condemnation

d. Eminent domain

19. What does the National Environmental Policy Act require federal agencies prepare for any development project that the federal agencies could prohibit or regulate?

a. A wetlands preservation plan

b. An environmental protection master plan

c. A master plan

d. An environmental impact statement

20. Pursuant to Florida real estate law, all known facts that are not readily observable by the buyer and that materially affect the value of residential real property must be disclosed to the buyer, except which, if any, of the following?

a. The fact that an occupant of real property is or has been infected with HIV

b. The fact that a homicide, suicide, or death occurred on the property more than three years ago

c. The fact that a homicide, suicide, or death occurred on the property during the past one year

d. None of the above.

21. John wants to put a clause in the deed that he is transferring to Lauren that might result in the reversion of the property to John. What should John place in the deed?

a. An affirmative covenant

b. A negative covenant

c. A condition

d. A conditional use clause

22. In case an item is scarce, but has no demand, the item would

a. Have a high market value

b. Have great functional utility

c. Command a high market price

d. Be essentially worthless

23. The value measured by the cost of building a property with current materials and labor refers to the property's

a. Replacement value

b. Reproduction value

c. Book value

d. Assessed value

24. The value that is paid for a property acquired by eminent domain refers to the property's

a. Book value

b. Scrap value

c. Salvage value

d. Condemnation value

25. Kathy is a broker who provides limited representation to both the buyer and the seller in a real estate transaction involving the sale of a condo. Kathy is

a. A designated agent

b. A dual agent

c. A transaction broker

d. A single agent of the buyer and of the seller

26. Which of the following is not a method used to estimate reproduction or replacement cost?

a. Square-foot method

b. Quantity survey method

c. Age-life method

d. Unit-in-in-place method

27. Pursuant to Florida real estate law, which of the following statements is false?

a. Each active broker must maintain an office, consisting of at least one enclosed room in a building of stationary construction.

b. Each active broker must maintain a sign on or about the entrance of her or his principal office and each branch office.

c. Each sign placed on or about the entrance of a broker's principal office must contain the name of the broker, but need not contain the trade name, if one exists.

d. At a minimum, the words "licensed real estate broker" or "lic. real estate broker" must appear on a broker's office entrance signs.

28. The process of ascertaining value by comparing and evaluating values obtained from different valuation approaches is called

a. Averaging the valuations

b. Adjustment

c. Reconciliation

d. Value correction

29. Which of the following statements is false?

a. A CMA may be prepared by a broker

b. A CMA only considers recently sold similar properties

c. A CMA may consider properties currently listed

d. A market data appraisal does not consider properties that are not sold

30. Which of the following is not a step that appraisers should follow in the process of developing an appraisal report?

a. Identify the relevant characteristics of the property

b. Determine data specific to the property

c. Collect, verify, and analyze the data

d. Consider the appraisal estimate that the client wishes to receive

31. Kathy is a Florida real estate broker who wishes to send a fax of an unsolicited advertisement to sell a home she listed to the top earning broker in her county. Under Florida law,

a. Kathy may send the fax to the other broker's main office.

b. Kathy may send the fax to the other broker's residential facsimile machine.

c. Kathy may not send the fax to the other broker.

d. Both a and b.

32. Fees that lenders charge to cover expenses of processing a loan are called

a. Origination fees

b. Discount fees

c. Advance fees

d. Point fees

33. PITI refers to

a. Property, interest, taxes, income

b. Principal, interest, taxes, income

c. Principal, interest, taxes, insurance

d. Principal, income, taxes, insurance

34. A partially amortized loan is

a. A loan under which the mortgage payments pay all of the interest due but not enough of the principal to fully pay off the loan at the end of the loan term

b. A loan wherein the payments are sufficient to pay off the entire loan by the end of the loan term

c. A loan wherein periodic payments consist of interest only

d. A loan wherein monthly installment payments do not cover all of the interest due

35. A final payment on a loan that is not fully amortized is a

a. NegAm payment

b. Level interest payment

c. Installment payment

d. Balloon payment

36. Evan is a sales associate who receives on Monday a good-faith deposit from a potential buyer for the purchase of a condo. Assuming no holidays during the week, Evan must deliver the deposit to his broker no later than the end of

a. Monday

b. Tuesday

c. Wednesday

d. Thursday

37. Which of the following statements is false?

a. Mortgage loans can be issued by the Consumer Financial Protection Bureau.

b. Mortgage loans can be issued by private mortgage insurers.

c. Mortgage loans can be insured by the FHA.

d. Mortgage loans can be insured by certain state-government entities.

38. Hannah purchases a building for $3,000,000 that has a useful life of 30 years and an anticipated residual value of $750,000. After 10 years, what is the value of the building, if by "value" we mean the original cost less accumulated straight-line depreciation?

a. $2,250,000

b. $2,000,000

c. $2,150,000

d. None of the above

39. A Florida broker must properly reconcile each of his or her escrow accounts

a. Every quarter

b. Every two months

c. Every month

d. Every two weeks

40. An advertisement submitted by a licensee that fails to reveal that the advertiser is an agent, not a principal, is called

a. An unprotected ad

b. A disapproved ad

c. A blind ad

d. A secret ad

41. A seller/owner who finances part of the purchase price of a property under a land installment contract is referred to as the

a. Vendor

b. Vendee

c. Grantor

d. Grantee

42. Which of the following statements is false about the VA-guaranteed loan program?

a. The VA does not make loans.

b. Approved lenders make the VA-guaranteed loans.

c. Persons who served only in the National Guard are not eligible.

d. The VA guarantee works much like PMI.

43. Which of the following statements is (are) false?

a. Under certain circumstances, a broker is allowed to place escrow funds in an interest-bearing account.

b. A broker is allowed to place escrow funds in an interest-bearing account only after obtaining written permission from all parties to the transaction.

c. A broker is allowed to place escrow funds in an interest-bearing account. Said escrow account *must* be in an insured account in a depository located and doing business in Florida.

d. All of the above statements are false.

44. What federal act is designed to prevent lenders, real estate agents, developers, title insurance companies, and other persons (such as appraisers and inspectors) who service the real estate settlement process from providing kickbacks or referral fees to each other, and from facilitating bait-and-switch tactics?

a. Truth-in-Lending Act

b. Real Estate Settlement Procedures Act

c. Equal Credit Opportunity Act

d. Consumer Financial Protection Act

45. A real estate licensee owes to clients a special relationship of utmost care, honesty, trust, and loyalty known as

a. A dual agent relationship

b. A subagent relationship

c. A fiduciary relationship

d. A power of attorney relationship

46. Charles purchased a home for $350,000 with a 6% fixed-rate, fully amortized 30-year loan in the principal amount of $312,208. He makes payments of $1,872 per month. What is the amount of unpaid principal on this loan after the first month's payment?

a. $310,336

b. $310,450

c. $311,429

d. None of the above

47. Subject to certain exceptions (such as regarding an earnest money deposit concerning a residential sale contract used by HUD in the sale of property owned by HUD), and if a broker receives conflicting demands for any trust funds being maintained in the broker's escrow account, which, if any, of the following actions may the broker not take?

a. File an interpleader.

b. File a motion for declaratory judgment.

c. Request the FREC to issue an escrow disbursement order

d. The broker may take any of the above actions

48. A buyer's agent who is a single agent

a. Owes fiduciary duties to both the seller and to the buyer

b. Does not owe a fiduciary duty to the buyer

c. Owes a duty to act fairly to the buyer but not to the seller

d. Owes a duty to act fairly to both the buyer and to the seller

49. A conflict of interest can exist

a. Regardless of any pecuniary gain

b. Regardless of any actual undue influence

c. Regardless of any evidence of wrongdoing or impropriety

d. All of the above

50. The unauthorized use of another's funds for one's own use is called

a. Conversion

b. Commingling

c. Ratification

d. Reconciliation

51. Kenny is a real estate salesperson who found a buyer for a home that sold for $750,000. Kenny's employing broker split the 5% commission for the sale with the listing broker. The agreement between Kenny his employing broker provides that Kenny receive 40% of his employing broker's commission on every sale Kenny procures. What is Kenny's commission on this transaction?

a. $18,750

b. $9,375

c. $15,000

d. none of the above

52. Brenda is a Florida real estate licensee who furnishes apartment rental lists to prospective renters for a $40 advance fee. Which of the following statements is false?

a. Brenda must provide such prospective tenant with a contract or receipt, which contract or receipt contains a provision for the repayment of any amount over 15 percent of the fee to the prospective tenant if the prospective tenant does not obtain a rental.

b. Brenda must provide such prospective tenant with a contract or receipt, which contract or receipt contains a provision for the repayment of any amount over 25 percent of the fee to the prospective tenant if the prospective tenant does not obtain a rental.

c. Brenda must provide such prospective tenant with a contract or receipt, which contract or receipt contains a provision for the repayment of any amount over 50 percent of the fee to the prospective tenant if the prospective tenant does not obtain a rental.

d. Brenda must provide such prospective tenant with a contract or receipt, which contract or receipt contains a provision for the repayment of any amount over 75 percent of the fee to the prospective tenant if the prospective tenant does not obtain a rental.

53. Which of the following statements is true?

91

a. Competitors are not guilty of price-fixing if they merely agree to *lower* prices and subsequently do so.

b. The mere appearance of an *implied* agreement between or among competitors is likely to be deemed a conspiracy to fix prices, to boycott a competitor, or to allocate market shares, if, subsequent to their communication, the parties act as if such an agreement had been reached.

c. Under the Sherman Act, the term "group action" refers to three or more persons agreeing to act.

d. An MLS may refuse membership to a broker who discounts fees beyond a certain point.

54. Which of the following statements is false?

a. All real estate agency compensation is subject to negotiation.

b. If an agent representing a buyer receives compensation indirectly from the seller, the agent is a dual agent.

c. By accepting or retaining the benefit of an act made by an unauthorized agent or by an agent who has exceeded his or her authority, a principal can create an agency by ratification.

d. An agent does not necessarily represent the person paying the commission.

55. The cost of a 35,000 square-foot lot is $30,800. What is the cost per square foot?

a. $1.14 (rounded)

b. $.86 (rounded)

c. $.75

d. None of the above

56. José is a sales associate who promises to pay the seller of a condo a percentage of José's commission if the sale is completed.

a. Being licensed as a sales associate and not as a broker, José may not under any circumstances share his commission with any party to the transaction.

b. Under Florida law, José may share 10% of his earned commission with the seller if he fully so informs all parties to the transaction.

c. Under Florida law, José may share no more than 15% of his earned commission with the seller even if he fully so informs all parties to the transaction.

d. None of the above choices is true.

57. If an agent is a co-owner of a property and the other owners authorize the agent to represent the property for sale,

a. The agent is a designated agent

b. The other owners may not revoke the agency

c. The agency is illegal because of a conflict of interest

d. The other owners may cancel the agency at any time because agency is a personal relationship based on trust and confidence

58. Margaret was involved in a real estate transaction in which she owed fiduciary duties to neither the buyer nor the seller. Margaret most likely was

a. The seller's agent

b. The buyer's agent

c. A dual agent

d. A transactional broker

59. Jennifer is a Florida sales associate who resigns from her employing broker on May 1 and becomes employed by a new broker on the same day. Jennifer must notify the FREC of the change no later than how many days after the change, on a form provided by the commission?

a. 5

b. 7

c. 10

d. 15

60. Antitrust laws impose restrictions on the conduct of real estate agents toward

a. Competitors

b. Clients

c. Customers

d. All of the above

61. A licensee must never recommend a particular inspection company (or other service)

a. That the licensee has used more than 5 times in the past 12 months

b. Unless the home inspection company is certified by the FHA

c. In which the licensee has a personal interest without full disclosure to the client

d. Unless the home inspection company is certified by the state in which the property being inspected is located

62. The Residential Lead-Based Paint Hazard Reduction Act requires that

a. Sellers must test for the presence of lead-based paint in residential dwelling units

b. Lead-based paint on walls of residential dwelling units must be removed before the unit can be sold or rented

c. Knowledge about whether lead-based paint was used in the dwelling must be disclosed

d. Lead water pipes must be replaced before the property can be sold or rented

63. In regard to the manner of creation, a contract may be

a. Express or implied

b. Express or unilateral

c. Express or bilateral

d. Express or executory

64. Ways in which a contract can typically be discharged do not include

a. By being fully performed

b. If the object or purpose of the contract becomes illegal

c. Inability of one party to profit from the agreement

d. If by the time the purpose of the contract is to be performed, it is impossible to do so

65. A listing agreement in which a seller reserves the right to sell the property to a buyer the seller procures without obligation to pay a commission to the seller's exclusive agent is called

a. An open listing

b. An exclusive right to sell listing

c. A net listing

d. An exclusive agency listing

66. Which, if any, of the following types of business entities may not register as a Florida real estate broker?

a. Limited liability partnerships

b. Business trusts

c. Limited liability companies

d. Each of the above may register as a Florida real estate broker.

67. Joel's Paint Shop has a lease under which Joel pays the landlord a fixed rent amount each month and the landlord pays all of the operating expenses of the premises. Joel's Paint Shop has what kind of lease?

a. Percentage lease

b. Net lease

c. Graduated lease

d. Fixed lease

68. A contract in which a property owner grants someone the right to purchase the property for a specified amount during a specified period of time is

a. A right of first refusal

b. A graduated lease

c. An option contract

d. A ground lease

69. A broker has the least protection with

a. A multiple listing

b. An open listing

c. An exclusive agency listing

d. An exclusive right to sell listing

70. Under Florida real estate law, an unlicensed personal assistant of a sales associate may not perform which of the following activities on behalf of the sales associate?

a. Receive, record, and deposit earnest money, security deposits and advanced rent.

b. Negotiate the rent for a condo.

c. Follow-up on loan commitments after a contract has been negotiated and generally secure the status reports on the loan progress.

d. Compute commission checks.

71. A lease under which the tenant pays a fixed rent plus the landlord's taxes, hazard insurance, and all maintenance costs not specifically reserved for the landlord's maintenance is called a

a. Triple net lease

b. Percentage lease

c. Graduated lease

d. Ground lease

72. Who is responsible for investigating complaints of violations by licensees of Chapter 475 of the Florida Statutes?

a. The Florida Real Estate Commission (FREC)

b. The Department of Business and Professional Regulation (DBPR)

c. The Division of Real Estate (DRE)

d. The Florida Attorney General

73. A lease for real property constitutes

a. A novation and a privity of chattel

b. A contract and a transfer of interests

c. An option with a contract

d. A document that must be in writing pursuant to the statute of frauds

74. Ryan applies for a sales associate license. Ryan's application will expire if he does not pass the Florida real estate sales associate exam within what period of time?

a. 3 years

b. 2 years

c. 1 year

d. 180 days

75. A contract cannot be valid unless

a. It is in writing

b. By its terms it can be fully performed within 2 years

c. It has a lawful object or purpose

d. None of the above

76. When requested to provide title insurance on a property, a title insurance company usually utilizes their own set of records called

a. A chain of title

b. A title plant

c. An abstract of title

d. An opinion of title

77. Payment to a claimant from the Florida Real Estate Recovery Fund based on a judgment against a broker or sales associate regarding a single real estate transaction may not exceed

a. $50,000

b. $100,000

c. $150,000

d. None of the above

78. Alex offers to buy Ned's cottage for $75,000. Ned writes back that he would take $85,000. Within this scenario is not

a. An offer

b. A rejection

c. A counteroffer

d. An acceptance

79. A legatee is

a. The receiver of real property by will

b. The receiver of real property by intestate succession

c. The receiver of personal property by will

d. The receiver of personal property by intestate succession

80. What type of deed is given at the foreclosure of a property, subsequent to a judgment of foreclosure of a money judgment against the owner or of a mortgage against the property?

a. General warranty deed

b. Special warranty deed

c. Sheriff's deed

d. Grant deed

81. Recording a deed to real property with the county recorder provides

a. Actual notice to subsequent purchasers or encumbrancers.

b. Constructive notice to subsequent purchasers or encumbrancers.

c. Acknowledgment to subsequent purchasers or encumbrancers.

d. Responsibility to subsequent purchasers or encumbrancers.

82. In Florida, whenever a landlord collects security deposit(s) or advance rent, the landlord or the landlord's agent must

a. Hold the total amount of such money in a separate non-interest-bearing account in a Florida banking institution for the benefit of the tenant(s)

b. Hold the total amount of such money in a separate interest-bearing account in a Florida banking institution for the benefit of the tenant(s)

c. Post a surety bond with the clerk of the circuit court in the county in which the dwelling unit is located in the total amount of the security deposits and advance rent the landlord or the landlord's agent holds on behalf of the tenants or $50,000, whichever is less

d. Either a, b, or c.

83. A lease with an option to purchase is a

a. Unilateral executory contract

b. Unilateral executed contract

c. Bilateral executory contract

d. Bilateral executed contract

84. Pursuant to which of the following laws must developers register subdivisions of 100 or more nonexempt lots or condominium units before offering such lots or condominium units for sale in interstate commerce?

a. Florida Fair Housing Act

b. Florida Deceptive and Unfair Trade Practices Act

c. Interstate Land Sales Full Disclosure Act

d. Florida Vacation Plan and Time-sharing Act

85. A purported agreement that is not, in fact, a contract and cannot be enforced by law is

a. An oral agreement

b. A voidable agreement

c. A valid agreement

d. A void agreement

86. Rent is typically paid in _____, in which case the buyer would be _____ for the portion of the month remaining after closing.

a. Advance, credited

b. Advance, debited

c. Arrears, credited

d. Arrears, debited

87. In Florida, a quarter-to-quarter tenancy may be terminated by either party

a. By giving not less than 90 days' notice prior to the end of any quarterly period

b. By giving not less than 60 days' notice prior to the end of any quarterly period

c. By giving not less than 30 days' notice prior to the end of any quarterly period

d. By giving not less than 15 days' notice prior to the end of any quarterly period

88. Unless the transaction is exempt, FIRPTA requires the buyer of real property to withhold what percent of the amount realized from the sale and to send that withheld amount to the IRS?

a. 15%

b. 10%

c. 5%

d. 3%

89. Examples of trust funds include

a. Earnest money deposits that a prospective purchaser gives to a broker as good-faith evidence of intention to complete the transaction

b. Rent from a broker's own real estate

c. A broker's real estate commissions

d. Security deposits from a broker's own real estate

90. *Shelley v. Kraemer* held that

a. Private racially-based restrictive covenants are invalid under the Fourteenth Amendment.

b. Only racially-based discrimination by federal, state, and local governments is prohibited under the Fourteenth Amendment.

c. Only racial- and religious-based discrimination by federal, state, and local governments is prohibited under the Fourteenth Amendment.

d. Only religious discrimination by federal, state, and local governments is prohibited under the Fourteenth Amendment.

91. Emily resides on property she owns that lies inside a Florida municipality. Under Florida homestead law, Emily may declare a homestead consisting of

a. Of one-half acre of contiguous land, upon which the exemption shall be limited to the land and the residence of Emily or the Emily's family

b. Of one acre of contiguous land, upon which the exemption shall be limited to the land and the residence of Emily or the Emily's family

c. Of 5 acres of contiguous land, upon which the exemption shall be limited to the residence of Emily or the Emily's family

d. Of 10 acres of contiguous land, upon which the exemption shall be limited to the residence of Emily or the Emily's family

92. Under Florida real estate law, the term "root of title" means

a. Any title transaction purporting to create or transfer the estate claimed by any person and which is the last title transaction to have been recorded at least 30 years prior to the time when marketability is being determined.

b. Any title transaction purporting to create or transfer the estate claimed by any person and which is the last title transaction to have been recorded at least 40 years prior to the time when marketability is being determined.

c. Any title transaction purporting to create or transfer the estate claimed by any person and which is the last title transaction to have been recorded at least 50 years prior to the time when marketability is being determined.

d. Any title transaction purporting to create or transfer the estate claimed by any person and which is the last title transaction to have been recorded at least 60 years prior to the time when marketability is being determined.

93. Anita purchased a home for $275,000 with a $55,000 down payment and a 5% fixed-rate loan. What is the amount of interest due for the first month?

a. $11,000

b. $10,000

c. $9,500

d. None of the above

94. Which, if any, of the following statements is (are) true?

a. A Florida real estate licensee must include in any written listing agreement a definite expiration date

b. A Florida real estate licensee must include in any written listing agreement the fee or commission

c. Both a and b.

d. Neither a nor b.

95. The Interstate Land Sales Full Disclosure Act is intended to

a. Encourage interstate subdivision sales

b. Encourage the subdivision and the development of state and federal land

c. Prevent unscrupulous subdividers from taking advantage of the public

d. Encourage the creation and sales of timeshares

96. Which, if any, of the following statements is false?

a. A lis pendens is a notice that provides constructive notice to potential purchasers or encumbrancers of a piece of real property of the pendency of a lawsuit in which an interest in that piece of real property is claimed.

b. Regarding mortgages, Florida is a title theory state.

c. Regarding mortgages, the borrower is referred to as the mortgagor.

d. A defeasance clause is a provision in a loan that states that when the loan debt has been fully paid, the lender must release the property from the lien so that legal title free from the lien will be owned by the borrower.

97. Florida does not impose transfer taxes associated with the transfer of real property on which if any of the following?

a. Documentary stamp tax on deeds and other instruments relating to real property or interests in real property.

b. Documentary stamp tax on promissory or nonnegotiable notes, written obligations to pay money, or assignments of wages or other compensation.

c. Intangible tax on new and assumed mortgages.

d. None of the above.

98. In a 1031 exchange, the term "boot" refers to

a. Like-kind property held for productive use received in the exchange

b. Cash or other not like-kind property received in the exchange

c. The falling out of the transaction due to irreconcilable differences

d. The rejection of recognition of the exchange by the IRS

99. José purchased a condo for $145,000, paying $29,000 cash, assuming the seller's outstanding mortgage of $72,500, and taking out a new mortgage in the amount of $43,500. The Florida intangible tax on all notes, bonds, and other obligations for payment of money that are secured by mortgages would be

a. $290

b. $232

c. $87

d. None of the above.

100. After completing the required post-licensing education during their initial license period, Florida real estate sales associates and brokers must complete how many hours of continuing education during each 2-year license period?

a. 14 for sales associates, 45 for brokers

b. 14 for sales associates, 14 for brokers

c. 45 for sales associates, 64 brokers

d. 16 for sales associates, 45 for brokers

ANSWERS TO PRACTICE EXAM #2:

Abbreviations used in this Practice Exam are:

DBPR — Department of Business and Professional Regulation
FAC — Florida Administrative Code
FREC — Florida Real Estate Commission
FS — Florida Statutes

1.   **b.** FS, 455.227(1)(t), states that disciplinary action may be taken against any licensee for failing to report in writing to the DBPR "within 30 days after the licensee is convicted or found guilty of, or entered a plea of nolo contendere or guilty to, regardless of adjudication, a crime in any jurisdiction."

2.   **a.** T2N, R3E, SBL&M refers to tiers, ranges, baselines, and meridians — gridlines in the U.S. government survey system.

3.   **c.** FS, 475.278(5)(a), defines the term "residential sale" as "the sale of improved residential property of four units or fewer, the sale of unimproved residential property intended for use of four units or fewer, or the sale of agricultural property of 10 acres or fewer."

4.   **c.** The key is highly adapted to the house is therefore a fixture; i.e., real property.

5.   **c.** FS, 475.02(1), states that the "commission shall consist of seven members who shall be appointed by the Governor, subject to confirmation by the Senate. Four members must be licensed brokers, each of whom has held an active license for the 5 years preceding appointment; one member must be a licensed broker or a licensed sales associate who has held an active license for the 2 years preceding appointment; and two members must be persons who are not, and have never been, brokers or sales associates. At least one member of the commission must be 60 years of age or older."

6.   **b.** Federal tax liens are general and involuntary liens.

7.   **d.** The most important feature distinguishing a joint tenancy from a tenancy in common is the right of survivorship.

8.   **b.** As distinguished from joint tenancy, tenancy in common may transfer their interest in the tenancy by will.

9.   **b.** FS, 475.23, provides that a "license shall cease to be in force whenever a broker changes her or his business address, a real estate school operating under a permit issued pursuant to s. 475.451 changes its business address, or a sales associate working for a broker or an instructor working for a real estate school changes employer. The licensee shall notify the commission of the change no later than 10 days after the change, on a form provided by the commission."

10.   **d.** An owner of a condominium need not worry about mowing the lawn, shoveling snow, weeding, landscaping, cleaning the pool, taking care of the roof, etc. The burden of accomplishing these tasks is the responsibility of the condominium homeowner's association or management board.

11.   **b.** A trade fixture is an object that a tenant attaches to real property for use in the tenant's trade or business. Trade fixtures differ from other fixtures in that, even though they are attached with some permanence to real property, they may be removed at the end of the tenancy of the business.

12.   **b.** FS, 455.02(1), states that any "member of the Armed Forces of the United States now or hereafter on active duty who, at the time of becoming such a member, was in good standing with any administrative board of the state and was entitled to practice or engage in his or her profession or vocation in the state shall be kept in good standing by such administrative board, without registering, paying dues or fees, or performing any other act on his or her part to be performed, as long as he or she is a member of the Armed Forces of the United States on active duty and for a period of 6 months after discharge from active duty as a member of the Armed Forces of the United States, if he or she is not engaged in his or her licensed profession or vocation in the private sector for profit."

13.   **a.** To exercise eminent domain, an appropriate governmental body must satisfy certain requirements, including that the property must be taken for the public good.

14.   **d.** Existing properties are said to be grandfathered in if they are granted a nonconforming use exception.

15.   **a.** The EPA defines brownfields as "real property, the expansion, redevelopment, or reuse of which may be complicated by the presence or potential presence of a hazardous substance, pollutant, or contaminant."

16.   **d.** FS, 475.278(2), states that a "transaction broker provides a limited form of representation to a buyer, a seller, or both in a real estate transaction but does not represent either in a fiduciary capacity or as a single agent." FS, 475.278(2)(a)-(g) states the duties of a real estate licensee involved in a transactional form of representation.

17.   **c.** Formaldehyde is a known cause of cancers in animals and possibly in humans that is extensively used to make building materials.

18.   **c.** Inverse condemnation is an action brought by property owners.

19.   **d.** The National Environmental Policy Act requires that federal agencies prepare an environmental impact statement (EIS) for any development project that a federal agency could prohibit or regulate, and any development project for which any portion is federally financed.

20.   **d.** FS, 689.25, provides that neither the "fact that an occupant of real property is infected or has been infected with human immunodeficiency virus or diagnosed with acquired immune deficiency syndrome" nor the "fact that a property was, or was at any time suspected to have been, the site of a homicide, suicide, or death" is a material fact that must be disclosed in a real estate transaction.

21.   **c.** Conditions (often called conditions subsequent) that are placed in a deed can have serious consequences if breached; namely, forfeiture of title.

22.   **d.** If an item is to have monetary value, it must possess all four of the elements of value to some degree. For example, an item might be scarce, but with no demand, in which case the scarce item would be essentially worthless (except perhaps in a nonmonetary sense).

23.   **a.** Replacement value is the value measured by the cost of building the property with current materials and labor.

24.   **d.** Condemnation value is the value that is paid for property acquired by eminent domain.

25.   **c.** FS, 475.01(1)(l), defines a transaction broker as "a broker who provides limited representation to a buyer, a seller, or both, in a real estate transaction, but does not represent either in a fiduciary capacity or as a single agent."

26. **c.** Primary methods used to estimate reproduction or replacement cost include the square-foot method, the quantity survey method, and the unit-in-place method.

27. **c.** FS, 475.22(1), provides that choices a, b, and d are correct. However, FS, 475.22(1), also provides that choice c is incorrect as follows: "Each sign must contain the name of the broker, together with the trade name, if any."

28. **c.** The process of ascertaining value by comparing and evaluating values obtained from different valuation approaches is called reconciliation.

29. **b.** A CMA typically will include data on three types of properties: (1) similar properties that have recently sold, (2) similar properties currently on the market, and (3) similar properties that have been on the market but whose listings have expired.

30. **d.** Appraisers are not permitted to take into consideration the appraisal estimate that clients wish to receive.

31. **c.** Pursuant to FS, 365.1657, it "is unlawful for any person to use a machine that electronically transmits facsimiles of documents through connection with a telephone network to transmit within this state unsolicited advertising material for the sale of any real property, goods, or services."

32. **a.** Fees that lenders charge to cover expenses of processing a loan are called origination fees.

33. **c.** PITI is an acronym for principal, interest, taxes, and insurance.

34. **a.** A partially amortized loan is a loan under which the mortgage payments pay all of the interest due but not enough of the principal to fully pay off the loan at the end of the loan term.

35. **d.** A balloon payment is a payment significantly greater than other payments, usually the final payment of a loan that is not fully amortized.

36. **b.** FAC, 61J2-14.009 provides that every "sales associate who receives any deposit … shall deliver the same to the broker or employer no later than the end of the next business day following receipt of the item to be deposited. Saturday, Sundays and legal holidays shall not be construed as business days."

37. **a.** Loans can be insured by private mortgage insurance (PMI), by the FHA, or by certain state-government entities.

38. **a.** Annual depreciation = (cost of property - residual value) ÷ useful life of property. Therefore, annual depreciation = ($3,000,000 - $750,000) ÷ 30 = $75,000.
Accumulated straight-line depreciation equals $75,000 × 10 = $750,000.
$3,000,000 - $750,000 = $2,250,000.

39. **c.** FAC, 61J2-14.012(2), provides as follows: "Once monthly, a broker shall cause to be made a written statement comparing the broker's total liability with the reconciled bank balance(s) of all trust accounts."

40. **c.** In addition to ensuring that no advertisement is submitted that is deceptive or discriminatory, most states prohibit brokers from running a blind ad, which is an advertisement that fails to reveal that the advertiser is an agent, not a principal.

41. **a.** A seller/owner who finances part of the purchase price of a property under a land installment contract is referred to as the vendor.

42. **c.** Persons who served in the National Guard or Selected Services are also eligible, usually with six years service.

43. **d.** FAC, 61J2-14.014 (1), provides that a "broker is allowed to place escrow funds in an interest-bearing account. The placement of escrow monies in an interest-bearing account, designation of the party who is to receive the interest, and the time the earned interest must be disbursed, must be done with the written permission of all the parties to the transaction. Said escrow account must be in an insured account in a depository located and doing business in Florida." Therefore, choices a, b, and c, are all true statements, making the final choice, d, false.

44. **b.** RESPA is a federal law designed to prevent lenders, real estate agents, developers, title insurance companies, and other persons (such as appraisers and inspectors) who service the real estate settlement process from providing kickbacks or referral fees to each other, and from facilitating bait-and-switch tactics.

45. **c.** A real estate licensee owes to clients a special relationship of utmost care, honesty, trust, and loyalty known as a fiduciary relationship.

46. **d.** $312,208 \times .06 \div 12 = \$1,561.04$ (first month's interest)
$1,872 - \$1,561.04 = \$310.96$ (first month's principal payment)
$312,208 - \$310.96 = \$311,897.04$ (principal balance after first month's payment).

47. **d.** FAC, 475.25(d)1, permits a broker to take any of the actions listed in choices a-c.

48. **d.** A buyer's agent who is a single agent owes a duty to act fairly to both the buyer and to the seller, but to the buyer, the buyer's agent also owes fiduciary duties.

49. **d.** A conflict of interest is a situation in which an individual or organization is involved in several *potentially* competing interests, creating a risk that one interest *might* unduly influence another interest.

50. **a.** Conversion is the unauthorized use of another's funds for one's own use.

51. **d.** Kenny's employing broker's commission is 50% of 5% of $750,000 = \$18,750$. Kenny's commission is 40% of $18,750 = \$7,500$.

52. **b.** FS, 475.453(1), provides that each "broker or sales associate who furnishes a rental information list to a prospective tenant, for a fee paid by the prospective tenant, shall provide such prospective tenant with a contract or receipt, which contract or receipt contains a provision for the repayment of any amount over 25 percent of the fee to the prospective tenant if the prospective tenant does not obtain a rental."

53. **b.** The mere appearance of an *implied* agreement between or among competitors is likely to be deemed a conspiracy to fix prices, to boycott a competitor, or to allocate market shares, if, subsequent to their communication, the parties act as if such an agreement had been reached.

54. **b.** The source of compensation does not determine agency representation. For example, an agent may represent only the buyer, but receive his or her entire commission as a commission split with the listing broker, in which case 100% of the buyer's agent commission would come (indirectly) from the seller.

55. **d.** 35,000 ft.² × (cost per square foot) = \$30,800.
Cost per square foot = $30,800 \div 35,000$ ft.² = \$.88 per square foot.

56. **b.** FAC, 61J2-10.028(2), provides that the sharing of brokerage compensation by a licensee, whether a sales associate or a broker, *with a party* to the real estate transaction is permissible as long as all parties to the transaction are given full disclosure of the sharing of the brokerage compensation. Note, however, that José's employing broker may disallow such a sharing of commissions by the broker's sales associates even though Florida law would otherwise permit the sharing of commissions with a party to the transaction.

57.   b. If an agent is a co-owner of a property and the other owners authorize the agent to represent the property for sale, then the other owners may not revoke the agency — which, under these circumstances, is referred to as an agency coupled with an interest.

58.   d. In Florida, a transactional broker provides limited representation to a buyer, a seller, or both, in a real estate transaction, but does not represent either in a fiduciary capacity or as a single agent, and neither the buyer nor the seller is responsible for the acts of a transactional broker.

59.   c. FS, 475.23, provides that whenever a sales associate working for a broker changes employer, the sales associate must notify the commission of the change no later than 10 days after the change, on a form provided by the commission.

60.   d. Activities prohibited by antitrust laws — such as price fixing, group boycotts, tying arrangements, and market allocation — can affect competitors, clients, and customers..

61.   c. A licensee must never recommend a particular inspection company (or other service) in which the licensee has a personal interest without full disclosure to the client.

62.   c. Pursuant to the Residential Lead-Based Paint Hazard Reduction Act, a seller (or lessor) of a residential dwelling unit built before 1978 must notify a buyer (or tenant) in writing about required disclosures for lead-based paint.

63.   a. In regard to the manner of creation, a contract may be express or implied. An express contract is one in which the parties declare their intention in words, whether orally or in writing. Nearly every real estate transaction must be express and, because of the statute of frauds, must be in writing. An implied contract is not written or spoken; it is implied by the actions of the parties.

64.   c. The inability of one party to profit from the agreement does not terminate the agreement or make it unenforceable.

65.   d. A listing agreement in which a seller reserves the right to sell the property to a buyer the seller procures without obligation to pay a commission to the seller's exclusive agent is called an exclusive agency listing. This question is an example of how important it is to read the entire question carefully, because without the last clause referencing an exclusive agent, the answer could be an open listing.

66.   b. FS, 475.15, provides that each "partnership, limited liability partnership, limited liability company, or corporation which acts as a broker shall register with the commission and shall renew the licenses or registrations of its members, officers, and directors for each license period." There is no provision for allowing business trusts to be registered as a real estate brokers.

67.   d. Under a fixed lease (also referred to as a gross lease), the tenant pays a fixed rental amount, and the landlord pays all of the operating expenses for the premises.

68.   c. In an option contract, the optionor grants the optionee the right to purchase property for a specific sum at any time during the option term without creating an obligation by the optionee to do so.

69.   b. An open listing agreement may be made by a seller to any number of brokers, though only one commission would be paid, going to the agent who first procurers an offer acceptable to the seller. The seller also reserves the right to sell the property to a buyer procured by the seller, without paying a commission to any broker. Furthermore, the sale of the property automatically terminates all outstanding open listing agreements for the property, without the need for notification on the part of the seller to the brokers to whom the seller gave an open listing. For these reasons, few agents are willing to spend time on open listings.

70.   **b.** FS, 475.01(1)(a), presents a list of activities brokers and sales associates may perform that require real estate licenses. One of those activities is the negotiating of rents. Choices a, c, and d are activities that unlicensed personal assistants may perform pursuant to the guideline "Permissible Activities of an Unlicensed Assistant" approved by the FREC, which, at the time of this writing, can be found at www.myfloridalicense.com/dbpr/re/documents/Permissibleactivitiesrev092009.pdf.

71.   **a.** A common variation on the net lease is the triple net lease, under which the tenant pays a fixed rent plus the landlord's property taxes, hazard insurance, and all maintenance costs not specifically reserved for the landlord's maintenance (such as repairs to the roof).

72.   **c.** FS, 475.021(1), provides that all "services concerning this chapter, including, but not limited to, recordkeeping services, examination services, legal services, and *investigative services*, and those services in chapter 455 necessary to perform the duties of this chapter shall be provided by the Division of Real Estate." (emphasis added)

73.   **b.** A lease has two distinct characteristics: a contract between landlord and tenant for payment of rent, maintenance of habitability, etc.; and a transfer of an estate in the real property leased.

74.   **b.** FS, 475.181(2), provides that an "application shall expire 2 years after the date received if the applicant does not pass the appropriate examination."

75.   **c.** The object or purpose of a contract is a thing that is agreed, on the part of the party receiving the consideration, to do or to forbear from doing. To be valid, the object or purpose of a contract must be lawful when the contract is made and possible when the contract is to be performed.

76.   **b.** A title plant is the duplicate set of records affecting title to properties in the area that are stored in-house by title insurance companies.

77.   **a.** FS, 475.484(3), provides that payment for claims arising out of the same transaction be limited to $50,000.

78.   **d.** Ned's counteroffer is both a rejection and a new offer.

79.   **c.** The receiver of personal property by will is known as a legatee.

80.   **c.** A sheriff's deed is a deed given at the foreclosure of a property, subsequent to a judgment of foreclosure of a money judgment against the owner or of a mortgage against the property.

81.   **b.** Recording provides access to information regarding ownership of the property and imparts constructive notice to subsequent purchasers or encumbrancers.

82.   **d.** FS, 83.49(1), provides that whenever a landlord or landlord's agent collects security deposit(s) or advance rent, the landlord or the landlord's agent must account for such money in one of three ways, as listed in choices a, b, or c.

83.   **c.** A lease-option is executory and bilateral because a lease is executory and bilateral.

84.   **c.** The Interstate Land Sales Full Disclosure Act is a federal law intended to protect consumers from fraud in the sale land. This Act requires developers to register subdivisions of 100 or more nonexempt lots or condominium units before offering such lots or condominium units for sale in interstate commerce.

85.   **d.** A void agreement is not considered a contract at all and cannot be enforced by law, such as an agreement to commit a crime.

86.   **a.** Rent is typically paid in advance, in which case the buyer would be credited for the portion of the month remaining after closing.

87.   **c.** FS, 83.57(2), provides that a quarter-to-quarter tenancy may be terminated by either party "by giving not less than 30 days' notice prior to the end of any quarterly period."

88.   **b.** FIRPTA requires the buyer of nonexempt real property to withhold 10% of the amount realized from the sale and to send that withheld amount to the IRS.

89.   **a.** Examples of *non*-trust funds include a broker's real estate commissions, rent and security deposits from a broker's own real estate, and any other funds personally owned by a broker.

90.   **a.** *Shelley v. Kraemer* held that private racially-based restrictive covenants are invalid under the Fourteenth Amendment.

91.   **a.** Article X, Section 4, of the Florida Constitution states that a homestead, if located within a municipality, shall consist of up to the extent of one-half acre of contiguous land, upon which the exemption shall be limited to the residence of the owner or the owner's family.

92.   **a.** FS, 712.01(2), states that "root of title" means "any title transaction purporting to create or transfer the estate claimed by any person and which is the last title transaction to have been recorded at least 30 years prior to the time when marketability is being determined. The effective date of the root of title is the date on which it was recorded."

93.   **d.** Loan amount = $275,000 - $55,000 = $220,000.
First month interest = ($220,000 × .05) ÷ 12 = $916.67.

94.   **c.** FS, 475.25(1)(r), provides that any written listing agreement must include a definite expiration date, description of the property, price and terms, fee or commission, and a proper signature of the principal(s).

95.   **c.** The federal Interstate Land Sales Full Disclosure Act is a consumer protection act intended to prevent unscrupulous subdividers from taking advantage of the public (e.g., by selling swamp land in Florida for residential development).

96.   **b.** FS, 697.02, provides that a "mortgage shall be held to be a specific lien on the property therein described, and not a conveyance of the legal title or of the right of possession." Therefore, in Florida, under a mortgage, the borrower retains legal title to the property purchased, whereas the lender receives a lien on the property — which makes Florida a lien theory state.

97.   **c.** Choice a is provided for by FS, 201.02. Choice b is provided for by FS, 201.08. Choice c is false because FS, 199.133, and FS, 199.145 provide for an intangible tax of 2 mils per dollar only on new mortgages, not on mortgages that are assumed.

98.   **b.** In a 1031 exchange, the term "boot" refers to cash or other not like-kind property received in the exchange.

99.   **c.** FS, 199.133, and FS, 199.145 provide for an intangible tax of 2 mils per dollar only on new mortgages, *not on mortgages that are assumed*. Therefore, the Florida intangible tax related to this transaction would be $0.002 × 43,500 = $87.

100.   **b.** FAC, 61J2-3.009(1)(a), provides that brokers and sales associates must complete a minimum of 14 hours of continuing education instruction during each license renewal period excluding the first renewal period of their current license.

PRACTICE EXAM #3:

Abbreviations used in this Practice Exam are:

DBPR — Department of Business and Professional Regulation
FAC — Florida Administrative Code
FREC — Florida Real Estate Commission
FS — Florida Statutes

1. Qualifications for licensure of a Florida real estate sales associate do not include

a. Being 18 years of age or older

b. Holding a high school diploma or its equivalent

c. Being a citizen of the United States

d. Submission of digital fingerprint data

2. A land owner has the right to have maintained both _____ from adjacent properties and _____ from the ground below.

a. Lateral support, littoral support

b. Subjacent support, lateral support

c. Subjacent support, chattel support

d. Lateral support, subjacent support

3. An employee of a owner-developer need not hold a real estate license to make sales of property owned by the owner-developer if

a. The employee's compensation is based in part on straight salary and in part on sales of real property made by the employee

b. The employee's compensation is based on a transactional basis

c. The employee's compensation is based solely on sales of real property made by the employee

d. The employee's compensation is based strictly on a salary

4. The original 13 states were surveyed using a version of which system?

a. Rectangular system

b. Recorded plat system

c. U.S. government survey system

d. Metes and bounds system

5. Florida Statutes, Chapter 475,

a. Provides that a Florida licensed real estate broker who is not a Florida certified or licensed real estate appraiser may provide valuation services for compensation, as long as the broker does not represent that he or she is a certified, licensed, or registered appraisers

b. Provides that a Florida licensed real estate sales associate who is not a Florida certified or licensed real estate appraiser may *not* provide valuation services for compensation

c. Provides that a Florida licensed real estate broker associate who is not a Florida certified or licensed real estate appraiser may *not* provide valuation services for compensation

d. Provides that all of the above are true

6. A landowner can claim

a. Unlimited rights to the airspace above his or her land

b. Only a reasonable amount of airspace above his or her land

c. No mineral rights that lay further than 100 feet beneath his or her land

d. No mineral rights that lay further than 200 feet beneath his or her life

7. Mechanics liens are _____ and _____ liens.

a. Specific, voluntary

b. General, involuntary

c. Specific, involuntary

d. General, voluntary

8. A lien is

a. A non-possessory right to use a portion of another property owner's land for a specific purpose, as for a right-of-way, without paying rent or being considered a trespasser

b. An encumbrance against real property that is used to secure a debt and that can, in most cases, be foreclosed.

c. A personal right to use property on a nonexclusive basis

d. A process whereby property passes to the state if the owner of the property dies intestate without heirs, or if the property becomes abandoned

9. The members of the FREC are appointed by

a. The Department of Business and Professional Regulation

b. The governor

c. An appointment committee whose members are appointed by the governor

d. The Real Estate Subcommittee of the Florida Senate

10. Last year Bob built a 3 foot high garden wall that extended onto Sally's property. The part of the wall that extended onto Sally's property is

a. A prescriptive easement

b. A lis pendens

c. An easement appurtenant

d. An encroachment

11. The primary economic characteristics of land include

a. Immobility, indestructibility, uniqueness

b. Scarcity, area preference, permanence of investment

c. Immobility, scarcity, cost

d. Uniqueness, location, immobility

12. Kathy is a sales associate employed by a broker who loses his license, causing Kathy's license

a. To be suspended

b. To be revoked

c. Status to be voluntary inactive

d. To become involuntarily inactive

13. What kind of tax is the main source of revenue for most local governments?

a. Income tax

b. Property tax

c. Sales tax

d. Special assessment

14. Inverse condemnation is brought by

a. Zoning boards

b. Planning commissions

c. Property owners

d. Boards of supervisors

15. Indoors, the concentration of _____ created by unvented gas space heaters, gas water heaters, fireplaces, and other sources of combustion can easily rise to a lethal level.

a. Radon

b. Carbon dioxide

c. Asbestos

d. Carbon monoxide

16. Which of the following statements is false under Florida real estate law?

a. Transaction brokers provide a limited form of nonfiduciary representation to a buyer, a seller, or both in a real estate transaction.

b. Without consideration of the related facts and circumstances, the mere payment or promise to pay compensation to a licensee does not determine whether an agency or transactional brokerage relationship exists between the licensee and a seller, landlord, buyer, or tenant.

c. Dual agency is permissible, but only with the written consent of all parties to the real estate transaction.

d. A single agent may represent either a buyer or a seller, but not both, in a real estate transaction

17. An easement that may be created if one uses another's land for a statutory period of time without permission is an

a. Easement by implication

b. Easement by necessity

c. Easement by prescription

d. Easement by reservation

18. Janet's customer, Susan, wants to buy a condo for $225,000. The best financing that Janet can find for Susan requires 18% down. How much would Susan have to come up with to handle the required down payment?

a. $45,000

b. $39,600

c. $40,500

d. None of the above

19. John, a known hermit, died without leaving a will. No heirs could be found. Eventually, a court ruled that title to John's home be transferred to the state. This is an example of

a. Eminent domain

b. Escheat

c. Progressive taxation

d. Condemnation

20. The Florida Brokerage Relationship Disclosure Act requires that

a. Single agency relationships must be disclosed in writing when dealing with residential real estate transactions

b. Transaction brokerage relationships must be disclosed in writing when dealing with residential real estate transactions

c. No brokerage relationships must be disclosed in writing when dealing with residential real estate transactions

d. Both a and c

21. A neighborhood grocery store that has been in business for 20 years is now, because of a re-zoning, in an area exclusively zoned for multi-unit residential buildings. In order to remain at the present location, the owners of the grocery store building should apply for

a. Nonconforming use

b. Variance

c. Conditional use

d. Spot zoning

22. Under the Comprehensive Environmental Response, Compensation, and Liability Act, which of the following parties would most likely not be responsible for the cleanup of a contaminated waste site?

a. The party who transported the waste to the site

b. The party who owned the site when the waste was dumped on the site

c. The party who purchased the site not knowing that it had been contaminated and who had not had the property inspected before purchasing

d. The party who inherited the site after the dumping occurred

23. The ability to sell, gift, or lease some interest in property refers to its

a. Transferability

b. Utility

c. Scarcity

d. Demand

24. The value that a property is carried on the owner's balance sheet, consisting of cost minus depreciation, refers to a property's

a. Assessed value

b. Appraised value

c. Book value

d. Investment value

25. Pursuant to Florida real estate law, all known facts that materially affect the value of residential real property and are not readily observable must be disclosed to the buyer by licensees involved in each of the following types of relationships, except

a. Single agent relationships

b. Transaction brokerage relationships

c. No brokerage relationships

d. None of the above

26. When using the income approach to appraisal, which of the following expenses is not deducted to obtain net income?

a. Hazard insurance

b. Income taxes

c. Maintenance costs

d. Reserves for replacements of building components

27. Henry is a transaction broker who provides limited representation to both the buyer and the seller in a real estate transaction involving the sale of a single-family home. Henry owes both the buyer and the seller each of the following duties, except

a. Using skill, care, and diligence in the transaction

b. Loyalty

c. Presenting all offers and counteroffers in a timely manner, unless a party has previously directed the licensee otherwise in writing

d. Disclosing all known facts that materially affect the value of the house and are not readily observable to the buyer

28. Loss in value of a property due to poor architectural style is referred to as

a. Economic obsolescence

b. Functional obsolescence

c. Physical obsolescence

d. Internal obsolescence

29. Federal rules require the use of a state licensed or certified appraiser for any federally related residential loan when the transaction value is

a. $100,000 or more

b. $200,000 or more

c. $250,000 or more

d. $500,000 or more

30. Using the gross rent multiplier approach, suppose the sales price of a condominium is $2,700,000 and the monthly rent is $9,000. What is the gross rent multiplier?

a. 200

b. 150

c. 300

d. None of the above

31. Pursuant to Florida real estate law, which of the following statements is false?

a. Each active broker must maintain a sign on or about the entrance of her or his principal office and each branch office.

b. Each active broker must maintain an office, consisting of at least one enclosed room in a building of stationary construction.

c. Each sign that a broker places on or about the entrance of his or her principal office must contain the name of the broker, together with the trade name, if any.

d. Each sign that a broker places on or about the entrance of his or her principal office must contain the name of the broker, but need not add the words "licensed real estate broker" or "lic. real estate broker."

32. Which of the following statements is false?

a. Points are used by lenders to measure discount charges.

b. Points are calculated based on the selling price.

c. Points are used by lenders to measure costs such as origination fees and private mortgage insurance premiums.

d. A point is equal to 1% of the loan amount.

33. A loan under which periodic payments consist of interest only is

a. A fully amortized loan

b. A term loan

c. A negative amortized loan

d. A level payment loan

34. In an adjustable-rate mortgage, though the _____ varies over the term of the loan, the _____ usually remains fixed over the loan term.

a. Fully indexed rate, margin

b. Margin, discounted rate

c. Margin, index

d. Index, margin

35. Which of the following statements is false?

a. A seller carry back loan is a loan or credit given by a seller of real property to the purchaser of that property.

b. Under a land installment contract, the seller does not convey legal title to the buyer until all installments are paid.

c. The buyer under a land installment contract is referred to as the vendee.

d. Upon the closing of a land installment contract, the seller conveys legal title to the buyer.

36. A brokerage firm is setting up a website. The firm name will appear in the top left of the home page of the site.

a. Point of contact information need not appear on the homepage as long as there is an internal link to a page, such as a "Contact Us" page, where point of contact information is displayed.

b. Point of contact information must be placed somewhere on the homepage of the website.

c. Point of contact information must be placed immediately below the firm name.

d. Point of contact information must be placed adjacent to or immediately above or below the firm name.

37. Benefits of FHA insured loans do not include

a. Relatively high LTVs

b. Down payments can be gifted by a relative

c. Relatively lenient PITI ratios (the standard guidelines being 41%)

d. The loans cannot have a prepayment penalty

38. A clause in a mortgage that states that upon default the lender has the option of declaring the entire balance of outstanding principal and interest due and payable immediately is called

a. A due-on-sale clause

b. A partial release clause

c. An acceleration clause

d. A defeasance clause

39. Kathy is a sales associate who receives on Monday a good-faith deposit from a potential buyer for the purchase of a single-family home. Kathy delivered the good-faith deposit to her broker the same day that she received the deposit. Assuming no holidays during the week, Kathy's broker must deposit the good-faith deposit Kathy received no later than the end of

a. Monday

b. Tuesday

c. Wednesday

d. Thursday

40. Under _____, the mortgagor retains both legal and equitable title, including exclusive possession and use of the property.

a. Title theory

b. Lien theory

c. Subrogation theory

d. Subordination theory

41. A deed of trust

a. Is a two-party instrument

b. Is a three-party instrument

c. Typically does not contain a power-of-sale clause

d. Typically provides for a lien to secure the loan without having an associated promissory note

42. An agent for a particular act or transaction is a _____. All other agents are _____.

a. Specific, general

b. Special, universal

c. Single, universal

d. Special, general

43. A broker may place and maintain up to what amount of personal or brokerage funds in a sales escrow account?

a. $250

b. $500

c. $1,000

d. $5,000

44. Real estate law concerns itself with conduct that real estate licensees ____ observe; codes of ethical conduct attempt to go beyond the law by defining what kinds of conduct agents ____ observe.

a. Should, most

b. Should, should

c. Must, should

d. Must, must

45. Which of the following statements is true?

a. A lender's asking whether an applicant is divorced is called steering.

b. Refusing to loan in a particular area is called blockbusting.

c. Directing people of protected classes from, or toward, particular areas is called redlining.

d. Representing that prices will decline, or crime increase, or other negative effects will occur because of the entrance of minorities into particular areas is called blockbusting or panic selling.

46. Under the Equal Credit Opportunity Act (ECOA), a loan applicant has the right to receive notification from the lender within how many days as to what action the lender has taken on a loan application.

117

a. 30

b. 15

c. 10

d. 5

47. Assuming that a broker's escrow account is an interest-bearing account, which of the following statements is (are) false?

a. Before the broker places escrow funds into the interest-bearing account, the broker must receive written permission of all parties to the transaction.

b. The broker may personally receive the interest on the escrow account if the broker has received written permission from all parties to the transaction to do so.

c. The interest-bearing account must be placed in a depository located in and doing business in Florida

d. All of the above statements are false.

48. Unless the statute of frauds requires the agency agreement to be in writing, an express agency agreement can be

a. Created by ratification

b. Created by an oral agreement

c. Created by implication

d. Created by estoppel

49. Which of the following statements is false?

a. A single agent is an agent of an agent.

b. A designated agent is an agent authorized by a real estate broker to represent a specific principal to the exclusion of all other agents in the brokerage.

c. A universal agent is an agent given power of attorney to act on behalf of a principal for an unlimited range of matters.

d. Ostensible agency is created when a principal intentionally, or by want of ordinary care, causes a third person to believe another to be his agent who is not actually employed by the principal.

50. A _____ is a situation in which an individual or organization is involved in several *potentially* competing interests, creating a risk that one interest *might* unduly influence another interest.

a. Pecuniary gain

b. Single agency

c. Conflict of interest

d. Designated agency

51. If the annual net operating income of a property is $74,000 and the capitalization rate is 7.5% per year, what would be the value of the property based on an income valuation of the property?

a. $986,667 (rounded)

b. $933,334 (rounded)

c. $98,667 (rounded)

d. None of the above

52. John is a Florida real estate broker who has received conflicting demands for trust funds from the buyer and seller of an office building. John must provide written notification to the FREC within how many days of the last party's demand?

a. 20

b. 15

c. 10

d. 5

53. Which of the following statements is false?

a. By accepting or retaining the benefit of an act made by an unauthorized agent or by an agent who has exceeded his or her authority, a principal can create an agency by ratification.

b. An agent may represent only the buyer, but receive compensation (indirectly) from the seller.

c. In some states, real estate agent compensation is fixed by law.

d. The source of compensation does not determine agency representation.

54. Bob is the listing agent for Susan's house. He signs a buyer agency agreement with Larry, who gives an offer for Susan's house. Bob is

a. A single agent

b. A transactional broker

c. A dual agent

d. An ostensible agent

55. A "red flag" in real estate is

a. A condition that should alert a reasonably attentive person of a potential problem that warrants further investigation

b. A natural hazards insurance policy

c. A basic homeowners warranty program

d. An exception that may be granted in cases where damage to the value of a property from the strict enforcement of zoning ordinances would far outweigh any benefit to be derived from enforcement

56. Sam is a Florida real estate licensee who furnished an apartment rental list to Julie for a $40 advance fee. Which of the following statements is (are) true?

a. A demand from Julie for the return of the fee, or any part thereof, must be made within 45 days following the day on which Sam contracted furnished the apartment rental list to Julie.

b. A demand from Julie for the return of the fee, or any part thereof, must be made within 15 days following the day on which Sam contracted furnished the apartment rental list to Julie.

c. If the rental information list provided by Sam to Julie is not current or accurate in any material respect, the full fee must be repaid to Julie upon demand.

d. Both a and c.

57. Megan's law is

a. A federal consumer protection law that requires certain land developers to register with the Consumer Financial Protection Bureau

b. An informal name for various federal and state laws that provide for the registration of sex offenders

c. A set of regulations that implement the Truth-in-Lending Act

d. A federal law that made enforceability of due-on-sale provisions a federal issue

58. Which of the following must be disclosed to buyers of single-family homes?

a. Additions to a house the seller made without the required permits

b. Known lead-based paint used in the home

c. Natural hazard zones that the property is known to lie in

d. All of the above

59. Martin is a Florida real estate associate who promises to pay a nonlicensed person a percentage of Martin's commission if the nonlicensed person refers Martin to a buyer of a home that Martin is trying to sell.

a. Martin may not share his commission with the unlicensed person.

b. Martin may share his commission with the unlicensed person as long as he receives permission to do so from his employing broker.

c. Martin may share his commission with the unlicensed person as long as he receives permission to do so from his employing broker and he fully informs all parties to the transaction of all facts relating to the sharing of his commission.

d. Martin may share his commission with the unlicensed person as long as (1) he receives permission to do so from his employing broker, (2) he fully informs all parties to the transaction of all facts relating to the sharing of his commission, and (3) he shares no more than 10% of his commission with the unlicensed person.

60. A bilateral contract is

a. A contract in which only one party gives a promise, leaving the other party with the opportunity to accept by some kind of performance.

b. A contract stated in words, written or oral.

c. A contract in which a promise given by one party is exchanged for a promise given by the other party.

d. A contract that has not yet been fully performed by one or both parties.

61. Compensation for broker representation of a seller's property

a. May be fixed by custom in each locale

b. May be fixed for members of a broker's professional organization

c. May be fixed by uniform practice in a given city

d. Is always subject to negotiation between client and broker

62. John's condo lease has a clause in it that provides for yearly increases in rent based on the Consumer Price Index. This clause in John's lease is called

a. A graduated clause

b. An escalator clause

c. A percentage clause

d. A net clause

63. A lease that provides the tenant with the right, but not the obligation, to purchase the leased property at a specified price within a specified period of time is a

a. Right of first refusal

b. Lease-purchase

c. Lease-option

d. Graduated-purchase

64. A real estate contract between an unemancipated minor and a competent adult can be voided

a. By the minor

b. By the adult

c. Only by mutual agreement of both parties

d. By no one

65. A clause in a purchase contract states: "If within 60 days of the expiration of this listing agreement, the property is sold to anyone to whom Broker or a cooperating broker showed the property during the listing term, Seller agrees to pay Broker the agreed-up on commission in full." This contract clause is referred to as a

a. Recovery clause

b. Liquidated damages clause

c. Safety clause

d. Ratification clause

66. A Florida real estate broker changes her address. The broker must notify the FREC of the change of address no later than how many days after the change, on a form provided by the commission?

a. 15

b. 10

c. 7

d. 5

67. Privity of estate is

a. A legal doctrine that states that a legally enforceable relationship exists between the persons who are parties to a contract

b. Personal property that has become real property through attachment

c. A legal doctrine that states that a legally enforceable relationship exists between the parties who hold interests in the same real property

d. A leasehold interest that lies between a primary lease and a sublease

68. The legal remedy of canceling a contract and restoring each party to the same position held before the contract was entered into is

a. Revocation

b. Specific performance

c. Rescission

d. Termination

69. Emily purchased a home from Bob on which Bob had an outstanding loan balance of $385,000 on April 20, the day that escrow closed. The interest rate on the loan was 5% and was payable with the loan payment on the first of each month. If Emily assumed Bob's loan, who should have paid whom in regard to proration of the interest and by how much if the interest on the loan is due after it has accrued?

a. Emily should have been paid $1,015.97

b. Bob should have been paid $1,015.97

c. neither Bob nor Emily should have paid the other anything

d. none of the above

70. Which of the following statements is false?

a. Each partner of a limited liability partnership registered as a broker must register as a broker.

b. Each member of any limited liability company registered as a broker must register as a broker.

c. Each officer of any corporation registered as a broker must register as a broker.

d. Each director of a partnership registered as a broker must register as a broker.

71. John and Joe agree to rob a bank and a split the take 50-50. Their agreement is

a. Voidable

b. Void

c. Valid

d. Enforceable

72. Under Florida real estate law, an unlicensed personal assistant of a sales associate may perform which of the following activities on behalf of the sales associate?

a. Gather information for an appraisal.

b. Handout objective, written information on a listing or rental.

c. Be at an open house to handout materials such as brochures.

d. All of the above.

73. The legal entitlement to be given the first chance to purchase a property at the same price, terms, and conditions as is offered to third parties if and when the property is put up for sale is called

a. An option

b. A lease-option

c. A right of first refusal

d. An entitlement option

74. The Florida Division of Real Estate

a. Does not have the power to investigate an anonymous complaint.

b. May investigate an anonymous complaint if the complaint is in writing and is legally sufficient, if the alleged violation of law or rules is substantial, and if the department has reason to believe, after preliminary inquiry, that the violations alleged in the complaint are true.

c. Does not have the power to investigate a complaint made by a confidential informant.

d. Both a and c.

75. A statement by a title insurance company of the condition of the title and of the terms and conditions upon which it is willing to issue a policy is called

a. A preliminary report

b. A title search

c. An abstract of title

d. A chain of title

76. Mutual consent is often referred to as

a. Duress

b. Voidable

c. Adequate consideration

d. A meeting of the minds

77. Julie successfully completes the educational requirements necessary to apply for a Florida sales associate license. Julie's successful education course completion will be considered invalid for licensure if she does not pass the licensing exam within what period of time?

a. 180 days

b. 1 year

c. 2 years

d. 3 years

78. A devisee is

a. The receiver of personal property by will

b. The receiver of real property by will

c. The receiver of personal property by intestate succession

d. The receiver of real property by intestate succession

79. A sheriff's deed contains

a. A covenant of seisin

b. A covenant against encumbrances

c. A covenant of quiet enjoyment

d. No covenant

80. A grantor executed a declaration in front of a notary public that states that the grantor's signature on the deed is genuine. This declaration is called

a. An acknowledgment

b. An affidavit

c. Constructive notice

d. Actual notice

81. Bob sold his condo to Sandra, closing date October 16. Bob had prepaid his monthly homeowner's fee of $465 on the first of the month. How much of the homeowner's fee must the buyer reimburse Bob for if a calendar year is used for the calculation and the closing day belongs to the buyer?

a. $232.50

b. $240

c. $225

d. None of the above

82. Three persons received three different judgments against the same real estate licensee for actions made by the licensee in the same real estate transaction. The maximum that these three claimants may receive from the Florida Real Estate Recovery Fund is

a. $50,000 in aggregate

b. $50,000 to each of the three claimants

c. A pro rata amount based on the amount of the judgments, up to a maximum of $150,000 in aggregate

d. None of the above

83. Mortgage interest is usually paid in _____, in which case the buyer would be _____ for the portion of the month before closing.

a. Advance, credited

b. Advance, debited

c. Arrears, credited

d. Arrears, debited

84. A landlord who collects a security deposit or advance rent from a tenant must within how many days after receipt of the advance rent or security deposit, give written notice to the tenant that includes disclosure of the advance rent or security deposit, indicating, among other things, where the advance rent and/or security deposit is being held or state that the landlord has posted a surety bond as provided by law, and whether interest is being paid on the funds held.

a. 30

b. 15

c. 10

d. 5

85. Related to the sale of real estate, which of the following is not required on form 1099-S?

a. Seller's name

b. Seller's Social Security number

c. Market value appraisal of the property transferred

d. Gross sale proceeds of the transfer

86. The two primary purposes of a security instrument, be it a mortgage or a deed of trust, are

a. To create the legal groundwork for the lender's right to foreclose and to establish the lender's priority among creditors

b. To create the legal groundwork for the lender's right to foreclose and to establish that the sale price was no greater than the market value appraisal

c. To create the legal groundwork for the lender's right to foreclose and establish the lender's right to transfer the mortgage without approval of the borrower

d. To establish the lender's priority among creditors and to establish that the sale price was no greater than the market value appraisal

87. In Florida, a tenancy at will is referred to as

a. An estate for years

b. An estate at sufferance

c. A tenancy without a specific term

d. A tenancy with a specific term

88. Properties acquired by banks through foreclosure are called

a. Real estate owned properties

b. Judicially foreclosed properties

c. Nonjudicial he foreclosed properties

d. Blighted properties

89. Examples of trust funds do not include

a. Interest (if any) on trust funds

b. Funding for a loan

c. Rent from a broker's own real estate

d. Rent or lease payments made by a client's tenants

90. Olivia was a cooperating broker who earned 6% on the first $100,000 of a $250,000 sale. The remainder of the commission went to the listing broker, Emily. If the total commission earned on the sale was $12,750, what percentage of the remaining $150,000 did Emily receive?

a. 4%

b. 4.5%

c. 5%

d. 5.5%

126

91. In Florida, a week-to-week tenancy may be terminated by either party

a. By giving not less than 15 days' notice prior to the end of any weekly period

b. By giving not less than 7 days' notice prior to the end of any weekly period

c. By giving not less than 5 days' notice prior to the end of any weekly period

d. By giving not less than 3 days' notice prior to the end of any weekly period

92. Florida homestead exemptions include an exemption for personal property up to the value of

a. $500

b. $1,000

c. $10,000

d. $50,000

93. The Federal Fair Housing Act does not prohibit

a. Representing that prices will decline, or crime increase, or other negative effects will occur because of the entrance of minorities into particular areas

b. Discriminatory access to multiple listing services

c. Retaliation against, or intimidation of, anyone making a fair-housing complaint

d. Discrimination in the sale or rental of a single-family house by an owner provided that the owner does not own or have any interest in more than three single family houses at any one time, and that the house is sold or rented without the use of a real estate broker, agent or salesperson or the facilities of any person in the business of selling or renting dwellings

94. In Florida, a title search need only go back to the last title transaction to have been recorded at least how many years prior to the time when marketability is being determined?

a. 75

b. 50

c. 30

d. 25

95. Choose the most complete answer: The Civil Rights Act of 1866 prohibits

a. Racial discrimination in all real property, commercial and residential

b. Racial and religious discrimination in all real property, commercial and residential

c. Racial discrimination in all residential real property

d. Racial discrimination in residential real properties consisting of 1-4 dwelling units

96. Which, if any, of the following statements is (are) true?

a. A Florida real estate licensee *must* include in any written listing agreement a description of the property

b. A Florida real estate licensee *must* include in any written listing agreement price and terms

c. Both a and b.

d. Neither a nor b.

97. Which of the following statements is false?

a. Florida is a lien theory state.

b. Regarding mortgages, the lender is referred to as the mortgagee.

c. A lis pendens is a notice that provides actual notice to potential purchasers or encumbrancers of a piece of real property of the pendency of a lawsuit in which an interest in that piece of real property is claimed.

d. A due-on-sale clause is a clause in the promissory note, the security instrument, or both that states that the lender has the right to accelerate the loan if the secured property is sold or some other interest in the property is transferred.

98. Which of the following statements is false?

a. A broker acting alone may choose not to do business with another broker.

b. It would be legal for a state to pass a law requiring brokers not to discount their commissions below 2% of sales price.

c. Under the Sherman Act, "group action" refers to two or more persons agreeing to act.

d. An MLS organization may not set fees or commission splits for its members.

99. Beth purchased a Florida condo for $150,000, paying $30,000 cash, assuming that seller's outstanding $74,000 mortgage, and taking out a new mortgage in the amount of $46,000. The documentary stamp tax on the notes resulting from this transaction would be

a. $420

b. $161

c. $259

d. None of the above

100. In Florida, liens on real property for property taxes attach to the property on

a. January 1 of the year the taxes were levied

b. March 1 of the year the taxes were levied

c. April 1 of the year the taxes were levied

d. November 1 of the year the taxes were levied

ANSWERS TO PRACTICE EXAM #3:

Abbreviations used in this Practice Exam are:

DBPR — Department of Business and Professional Regulation
FAC — Florida Administrative Code
FREC — Florida Real Estate Commission
FS — Florida Statutes

1.   **c.** FAC, 61J2-2.027 states that answers a, b, and d are required for licensure. There is no requirement of being a U.S. citizen or a Florida resident.

2.   **d.** A landowner has the right to have maintained both lateral support from adjacent properties and subjacent support from the ground below.

3.   **d.** FS, 475.011(2), defines "owner-developer" and states that the exemption of employees of owner-developers only applies if the employees' compensation is based strictly on a salary, and not in part on sales made by the employees.

4.   **d.** The oldest method of surveying in the United States is the metes and bounds system, which was used by the original 13 states.

5.   **a.** FS, 475.612(2), provides that a Florida licensed real estate broker, sales associate, or broker associate who is not a Florida certified or licensed real estate appraiser *may* provide valuation services for compensation, as long as they do not represent themselves as certified, licensed, or registered appraisers.

6.   **b.** Contemporary law gives the landowner only a "reasonable" amount of airspace above his or her land.

7.   **c.** Mechanics liens are specific and involuntary liens.

8.   **b.** A lien is an encumbrance against real property that is used to secure a debt and that can, in most cases, be foreclosed.

9.   **b.** FS, 475.02(1), states that the "commission shall consist of seven members who shall be appointed by the Governor, subject to confirmation by the Senate."

10.   **d.** An encroachment is a thing affixed under, on, or above the land of another without permission.

11.   **b.** The primary economic characteristics of land are area preference (situs), scarcity, permanence of investment (fixity or duration), and the ability of improvements to modify the value.

12.   **d.** FS, 475.31(1), provides that an "order revoking or suspending the license of a broker shall automatically cause the licenses of all sales associates and broker associates registered with the broker…to become involuntarily inactive, while the license of the broker is inoperative or until new employment or connection is secured."

13.   **b.** Property taxes are the main source of revenue for most local governments.

14.   **c.** Inverse condemnation is a judicial or administrative action brought by a landowner to force the condemnation of the landowner's land where nearby condemned land or land used for public purposes (such as for noisy airports) severely reduces the value of the landowner's land.

15. **d.** Indoors, the concentration of carbon monoxide created by unvented gas space heaters, gas water heaters, fireplaces, and other sources of combustion can easily rise to a lethal level.

16. **c.** FS, 475.272(1), disallows dual agency in the state of Florida.

17. **c.** An easement by prescription can be created under certain circumstances, such as when one uses another's land for a statutory period of time without permission.

18. **c.** $\$225,000 \times .18 = \$40,500$.

19. **b.** Escheat is a process whereby property passes to the state (or in some cases the county) if a person owning the property dies intestate without heirs.

20. **d.** FS, 475.278(3) and (4), require that single agency relationships and no brokerage relationships must be disclosed in writing when dealing with residential real estate transactions. There is no requirement that a transactional brokerage relationship must be disclosed in writing unless a single agency relationship is being changed to a transaction brokerage relationship, in which case a written consent of the principal must be obtained. FS, 278(3)(b)2.

21. **a.** Nonconforming use refers to an exception for areas that are zoned for the first time or that are rezoned and where established property uses that previously were permitted do not conform to the new zoning requirements.

22. **d.** A person who acquires a contaminated property by inheritance or bequest *after* it was contaminated is considered an innocent landowner.

23. **a.** The ability to sell, gift, or lease some interest in property refers to its transferability.

24. **c.** Book value is the value at which a property is carried on the owner's balance sheet, consisting of cost minus book depreciation.

25. **d.** FS, 475.278, requires that licensees involved in single agent relationships, transaction brokerage relationships, and no brokerage relationships disclose all known facts that materially affect the value of residential real property and are not readily observable to the buyer.

26. **b.** Examples of expenses that are not deducted to obtain net income include mortgage payments and taxes on income.

27. **b.** FS, 475.278(2), lists the duties of a transaction broker. These duties include each of those listed in choices a, c, and d, but not choice b, which is one of the fiduciary duties owed by a single agent to a single agent's principal.

28. **b.** Loss in value of a property due to poor architectural style is referred to as functional obsolescence.

29. **c.** Federal rules require the use of a state licensed or certified appraiser for any federally related residential loan when the transaction value is $250,000 or more.

30. **c.** $\$2,700,000 \div \$9,000 = 300$.

31. **d.** FS, 475.22(1), provides that choices a, b, and c are correct. However, FS, 475.22(1), also provides that choice d is incorrect as follows: "At a minimum, the words 'licensed real estate broker' or 'lic. real estate broker' must appear on the office entrance signs.

32. **b.** Points are calculated based on the loan amount, not on the selling price.

33. **b.** A loan under which periodic payments consist of interest only is a term loan (also referred to as a straight loan or an interest-only loan).

34. **d.** In an adjustable-rate mortgage, though the index varies over the term of the loan, the margin usually remains fixed over the loan term.

35. **d.** Upon the closing of a land installment contract, the buyer takes immediate possession of the property, but the seller does not convey legal title to the buyer until all installments are paid.

36. **d.** FAC, 61J2-10.25(3)(a), provides that when "advertising on a site on the Internet, the brokerage firm name… shall be placed adjacent to or immediately above or below the point of contact information. 'Point of contact information' refers to any means by which to contact the brokerage firm or individual licensee including mailing address(es), physical street address(es), e-mail address(es), telephone number(s) or facsimile telephone number(s)."

37. **c.** FHA does have relatively lenient PITI ratios, but the standard guideline is 29%; 31% max.

38. **c.** An acceleration clause states that, upon default (such as failure to make payments as agreed) or a violation of other conditions (such as failure to maintain proper insurance), the lender has the option of declaring the entire balance of outstanding principal and interest due and payable immediately.

39. **d.** FAC, 61J2-14.010, states that every broker who receives from a sales associate a good-faith deposit must "immediately" deposit the good-faith deposit. FAC, 61J2-14.008(3), provides that the word "immediately" means "the placement of a deposit in an escrow account no later than the end of the third business day following receipt of the item to be deposited." FAC, 61J2-14.009, provides that receipt "by a sales associate or any other representative of the brokerage firm constitutes receipt by the broker." *Therefore, even though Kathy's broker did not have the good-faith deposit in hand until Tuesday, Kathy's broker nevertheless was in "receipt" of the good-faith deposit on Monday, pursuant to FAC, 61J2-14.009.*

40. **b.** Under lien theory, the mortgagor retains both legal and equitable title, including exclusive possession and use of the property.

41. **b.** A deed of trust is a three-party instrument.

42. **d.** An agent for a particular act or transaction is a special agent. All other agents are general agents.

43. **c.** FAC, 61J2-14.010(2), provides as follows: "A broker may place and maintain up to $1,000 of personal or brokerage funds per each *sales* escrow account. A broker may place and maintain up to $5,000 of personal or brokerage funds per each *property management* escrow account." (emphasis added)

44. **c.** Real estate law concerns itself with conduct that real estate licensees *must* observe; codes of ethical conduct attempt to go beyond the law by defining what kinds of conduct agents *should* observe.

45. **d.** Representing that prices will decline, or crime increase, or other negative effects will occur because of the entrance of minorities into particular areas is called blockbusting or panic selling.

46. **a.** Under ECOA, an applicant has the right to receive notification from the lender within 30 days as to what action the lender has taken on a loan application.

47.   **d.** FAC, 61J2-14.014 (1), provides that a "broker is allowed to place escrow funds in an interest-bearing account. The placement of escrow monies in an interest-bearing account, *designation of the party who is to receive the interest*, and the time the earned interest must be disbursed, must be done with the written permission of all the parties to the transaction. Said escrow account must be in an insured account in a depository located and doing business in Florida." (emphasis added) Therefore, choices a, b, and c, are all true statements, making the final choice, d, false.

48.   **b.** Unless the statute of frauds requires that the agreement be in writing, an express agency agreement can be oral.

49.   **a.** A single agent is an agent who represents only one party in a given transaction.

50.   **c.** A conflict of interest is a situation in which an individual or organization is involved in several *potentially* competing interests, creating a risk that one interest *might* unduly influence another interest.

51.   **a.** $74,000 ÷ 7.5% = $986,667 (rounded).

52.   **b.** FAC, 61J2-10.032(1)(a), provides that a "real estate broker, upon receiving conflicting demands for any trust funds being maintained in the broker's escrow account, must provide written notification to the Commission within 15 business days of the last party's demand."

53.   **c.** All real estate agency compensation is subject to negotiation — it is not fixed by law or custom.

54.   **c.** Susan and Larry are both clients of Bob, making Bob a dual agent, which is an illegal form of agency under Florida real estate law.

55.   **a.** A "red flag" is a property condition that should alert a reasonably attentive person of a potential problem that warrants further investigation.

56.   **c.** Both choices a and b are false, and choice c is true, pursuant to FS, 475.453(1), which states as follows: "If the rental information list provided by the broker or sales associate to a prospective tenant is not current or accurate in any material respect, the full fee shall be repaid to the prospective tenant upon demand. A demand from the prospective tenant for the return of the fee, or any part thereof, shall be made within 30 days following the day on which the real estate broker or sales associate has contracted to perform services to the prospective tenant."

57.   **b.** Megan's law is an informal name for various federal and state laws that provide for the registration of sex offenders and for the making available to the public information regarding the location of these offenders.

58.   **d.** All of the matters stated in a-c are material facts that must be disclosed.

59.   **a.** FS, 475.25(1)(h), provides that a licensee may not share his or her real estate compensation with an unlicensed person. Note, however, that FAC, 61J2-10.028(2), provides that the sharing of brokerage compensation by a licensee *with a party* to the real estate transaction is permissible as an exception to FS, 475.25(1)(h), as long as all parties to the transaction are given full disclosure of the sharing of the brokerage compensation.

60.   **c.** A bilateral contract is a contract in which a promise given by one party is exchanged for a promise given by the other party.

61.   **d.** For all listing agreements, compensation of the broker is subject to negotiation — it is not fixed by law or custom.

62. **b.** An escalator clause in a lease is a clause that provides for a periodic increase in rent in an amount based on something not in control of either the tenant or the landlord, such as the Consumer Price Index.

63. **c.** A lease with an option to purchase (also referred to as a lease-option) provides that the lessee has the right to purchase the property at the specified price and terms any time prior to a specified date, but has no obligation to do so.

64. **a.** A real estate contract between an unemancipated minor and a competent adult can be voided by the minor (or the minor's guardian) but not unilaterally by the adult.

65. **c.** A safety clause is a provision in a listing agreement, providing that the broker will earn the full commission if the property is sold within a specified number of days after the termination of the listing to a buyer with whom the broker has dealt in certain specified ways regarding the property.

66. **b.** FS, 475.23, provides that whenever a broker changes his or her business address, the broker must notify the commission of the change no later than 10 days after the change, on a form provided by the commission.

67. **c.** Privity of estate is a legal doctrine that states that a legally enforceable relationship exists between the parties who hold interests in the same real property.

68. **c.** Rescission extinguishes a contract and returns each party to the position it was in immediately prior to the formation of the contract.

69. **a.** The seller, Bob, owned the home for 19 days before closing — 19 days for which he had not paid the interest on the loan as of the closing of escrow. Emily should, therefore, have been credited for 19 day's interest.

The annual interest on the loan was 5%, and $385,000 was the loan balance on which interest would be paid by Emily (who assumed the loan) on May 1. Figured on an *annual* basis, interest of 5% on $385,000 = $19,250, so to obtain the *daily* interest amount for each day of April we divide $19,250 by 360 (using a statutory year) to get $53.4722. [Note that in proration problems it is best to use at least four numbers after the decimal point until you get to the final answer, which can be rounded off.] Because Emily should have been credited for 19 days, her credit should have been 19 × $53.4722 = $1,015.97.

70. **a.** FS, 475.15, provides that "if the partnership is a limited partnership, only the general partners must be licensed brokers or brokerage corporations."

71. **b.** An agreement to commit a crime is void.

72. **d.** Choices a, b, c, and d are activities that unlicensed personal assistants may perform pursuant to the guideline "Permissible Activities of an Unlicensed Assistant" approved by the FREC, which, at the time of this writing, can be found at www.myfloridalicense.com/dbpr/re/documents/Permissibleactivitiesrev092009.pdf.

73. **c.** A right of first refusal is the right to be given the first chance to purchase a property at the same price, terms, and conditions as is offered to third parties if and when the property is put up for sale.

74. **b.** FS, 475.021(1), provides that all "services concerning this chapter, including, but not limited to, recordkeeping services, examination services, legal services, and *investigative services, and those services in chapter 455* necessary to perform the duties of this chapter shall be provided by the Division of Real Estate." (emphasis added) Additionally, FS, 455.225(1)(a), provides that the "department may investigate an *anonymous complaint* if the complaint is in writing and is legally sufficient, if the alleged violation of law or rules is substantial, and if the department has reason to believe, after preliminary inquiry, that the violations alleged in the complaint are true. The department may investigate a complaint made by a *confidential informant* if the complaint is legally sufficient, if the alleged violation of law or rule is substantial, and if the department has reason to believe, after preliminary inquiry, that the allegations of the complainant are true." (emphasis added)

75. **a.** A preliminary report is a statement by a title insurance company of the condition of the title and of the terms and conditions upon which it is willing to issue a policy.

76. **d.** Mutual consent is often referred to as a "meeting of the minds" and is usually evidenced by an offer of one party that manifests contractual intention and by an acceptance by the other party.

77. **c.** FS 475.181(2), provides that "if an applicant does not pass the licensing examination within 2 years after the successful course completion date, the applicant's successful course completion is invalid for licensure."

78. **b.** The receiver of real property by will is known as a devisee.

79. **d.** A sheriff's deed contains no warranties and transfers only the former owner's interest, if any, in the property.

80. **a.** An acknowledgment is a formal declaration made by the grantor before a duly authorized public official (such as a notary public), that states that the grantor voluntarily signed the deed and that the signature on the deed is the grantor's signature.

81. **b.** The number of days the buyer must reimburse Bob for is 31-15 = 16. The daily rate of the homeowner's fee for October was $465 \div 31 = \$15$. Therefore the buyer must reimburse Bob in an amount of $\$15 \times 16 = \$240$.

82. **a.** FS, 475.484(3), states that payments "for claims arising out of the same transaction shall be limited, in the aggregate, to $50,000, regardless of the number of claimants or parcels of real estate involved in the transaction."

83. **c.** Mortgage interest is usually paid in arrears, in which case the buyer would be credited for the portion of the month before closing.

84. **a.** FS, 83.49(2), provides that a landlord who collects a security deposit or advance rent from a tenant must, within 30 days after receipt of the advance rent or security deposit, give written notice to the tenant that includes, among other things, where the advance rent and/or secure deposit is being held or state that the landlord has posted a surety bond as provided by law, and whether interest is being paid on the funds held

85. **c.** The IRS requires escrow agents to report every sale of real estate on Form 1099-S, giving the seller's name, Social Security number, and the gross sale proceeds. A market value appraisal of the property is not required.

86. **a.** The two primary purposes of a security instrument, be it a mortgage or a deed of trust, are (1) to create the legal groundwork for the lender's right to foreclose and (2) to establish the lender's priority among creditors.

87. **c.** In Florida, a tenancy at will is referred to as a tenancy without a specific term, as defined in FS, 83.46(2) or (3).

88. **a.** Bank-owned properties acquired through foreclosure are called real estate owned (REO) properties.

89. **c.** Examples of non-trust funds include a broker's real estate commissions, rent and security deposits from a broker's own real estate, and any other funds personally owned by a broker.

90. **b.** Olivia received 6% of $100,000 = $6,000.
Therefore, Emily received $12,750 - $6,000 = $6,750.
$6,750 ÷ $150,000 = .045 = 4½%.

91. **b.** FS, 83.57(4), provides that a week-to-week tenancy may be terminated by either party "by giving not less than 7 days' notice prior to the end of any weekly period."

92. **b.** Article X, Section 4, of the Florida Constitution states that a homestead exemption exists for "personal property to the value of one thousand dollars."

93. **d.** The Federal Fair Housing Act does not prohibit discrimination in the sale or rental of a single-family house by an owner provided that the owner does not own or have any interest in more than three single family houses at any one time, and that the house is sold or rented without the use of a real estate broker, agent or salesperson or the facilities of any person in the business of selling or renting dwellings.

94. **c.** FS, 712.02, provides that any "person having the legal capacity to own land in this state, who, alone or together with her or his predecessors in title, has been vested with any estate in land of record for 30 years or more, shall have a marketable record title to such estate in said land, which shall be free and clear of all claims except the matters set forth as exceptions to marketability in s. 712.03."

95. **a.** In the 1968 landmark case *Jones v. Mayer*, the United States Supreme Court held that the Civil Rights Act of 1866 prohibited all racial discrimination, whether private or public, in the sale or rental of either real or personal property.

96. **c.** FS, 475.25(1)(r), provides that any written listing agreement must include a definite expiration date, description of the property, price and terms, fee or commission, and a proper signature of the principal(s).

97. **c.** A lis pendens is a notice that provides actual *constructive* notice to potential purchasers or encumbrancers of a piece of real property of the pendency of a lawsuit in which an interest in that piece of real property is claimed. Choice a is correct because FS, 697.02, provides that a "mortgage shall be held to be a specific lien on the property therein described, and not a conveyance of the legal title or of the right of possession." Therefore, in Florida, under a mortgage, the borrower retains legal title to the property purchased, whereas the lender receives a lien on the property — which makes Florida a lien theory state.

98. **b.** Federal antitrust-price-fixing law makes it illegal for any state agency or any trade organization to set commission rates for real estate transactions.

99. **a.** FS, 201.08, provides for a documentary stamp tax on promissory notes in the amount of $.35 per $100 or fraction thereof. This applies to both notes for new mortgages as well as on notes for assumed mortgages. Beth's assumed and new mortgages total $120,000. $120,000 ÷ $100 = 1,200. Therefore, the documentary stamp tax on the promissory notes related to this transaction is 1,200 × $.35 = $420.

100. **a.** FS, 197.122(1), provides that all "taxes imposed pursuant to the State Constitution and laws of this state shall be a first lien, superior to all other liens, on any property against which the taxes have been assessed and shall continue in full force from January 1 of the year the taxes were levied until discharged."

PRACTICE EXAM #4:

Abbreviations used in this Practice Exam are:

DBPR — Department of Business and Professional Regulation
FAC — Florida Administrative Code
FREC — Florida Real Estate Commission
FS — Florida Statutes

1. Qualifications for a Florida real estate license include

a. Possessing a Social Security number

b. Being a U.S. citizen

c. Being a Florida resident

d. Both a and b

2. The most important feature that distinguishes personal property from real property is its

a. Location

b. Cost

c. Ability to be moved

d. Situs

3. Any Florida resident real estate licensee who becomes a nonresident must, within how many days, notify the FREC of the change in residency and comply with nonresident requirements.

a. 60

b. 45

c. 30

d. 15

4. The SW¼ of the SW¼ of the NW¼ of Section 10 of Baker Township contains how many acres?

a. 80

b. 40

c. 160

d. 10

5. Florida Statutes, Chapter 177, defines "subdivision" as the division of land into how many lots, parcels, tracts, tiers, blocks, sites, units, or any other division of land?

a. 2

b. 3

c. 4

d. 5

6. A lien that is created by operation of law is

a. A voluntary lien

b. A specific lien

c. A general lien

d. An involuntary lien

7. Special assessment liens are _____ and _____ liens.

a. Specific, involuntary

b. General, involuntary

c. Specific, voluntary

d. General, voluntary

8. Most subdivisions use which legal land description?

a. Lot, block and tract system

b. Rectangular survey system

c. U.S. government survey system

d. Metes and bounds system

9. Any real estate license that has been involuntarily inactive for more than how long shall automatically expire, thereby becoming null and void?

a. 1 year

b. 18 months

c. 2 years

d. 3 years

10. If a person who benefits from an easement acquires the servient tenement, the easement

a. Becomes an easement in gross

b. Becomes an encroachment

c. Remains in effect but only as against future purchasers of the property

d. Is terminated

11. A thing affixed under, on, or above the land of another without permission is called

a. An easement by prescription

b. An easement appurtenant

c. A license to use

d. An encroachment

12. A sales associate's employing broker changes his or her address. Until the FREC is notified of the change of address and the broker is properly registered, the sales associate's license

a. Is unaffected

b. Ceases to be in force

c. Is suspended

d. Is revoked

13. To exercise eminent domain, an appropriate governmental body must satisfy certain requirements, including

a. That the owner must be paid a just compensation

b. That the governmental body must pay at least 110% of the property's assessed value

c. That the governmental body demonstrate that the taking will result in an increase in the property's fair market value

d. That the governmental body must demonstrate that the property was not used in conformance with existing zoning laws

14. Police power is not used to establish

a. Deed restrictions

b. Zoning codes

c. Subdivision regulations

d. Building codes

15. What federal law was designed to ensure that the parties responsible for polluting a site would be held responsible for its cleanup?

a. Coastal Zone Management Act

b. Clean Water Act

c. Comprehensive Environmental Response, Compensation, and Liability Act

d. Brownfields Revitalization Act

16. A Florida transaction broker first contacted by a seller owes fiduciary duties to

a. The seller

b. The buyer

c. Neither the seller nor the buyer

d. Both the seller and the buyer

17. In zoning, a strip of land to separate, or to ease the transition from, one use to another is referred to as a

a. Variance zone

b. Brownfield zone

c. Conditional use zone

d. Buffer zone

18. What is it that may be placed in a deed that could result in the reversion of title to the grantor?

a. Affirmative covenants

b. Subsequent use clauses

c. Conditions

d. Negative covenants

19. What is the value of a property based on the following information?
Estimated annual gross income: $95,000
Vacancies and uncollectible rents: 7%
Annual maintenance expenses and utilities: $10,000
Annual property taxes: $9,500
Annual insurances: $1,500
Monthly mortgage payment: $2,500
Capitalization rate: 9.5%

a. $393,159 (rounded)

b. $708,947 (rounded)

c. $778,947 (rounded)

d. None of the above

20. In Florida, the three roles that a real estate licensee may assume with principles and/or customers include each of the following, except

a. Single agency relationship

b. No brokerage relationship

c. Transaction brokerage relationship

d. Dual agency relationship

21. The first federal law that protected persons against racial discrimination in the lease or sale of real property was

a. Civil Rights Act of 1866

b. Federal Fair Housing Act

c. *Shelley v. Kraemer*

d. *Jones v. Jones*

22. Inclusionary zoning refers to

a. City and county zoning ordinances that require builders to set aside a given portion of new construction for people of low to moderate incomes

b. An exception for areas that are zoned for the first time or that are rezoned and where established property uses that previously were permitted to not conform to the new zoning requirements

c. An exception for special uses such as churches, schools, and hospitals that wish to locate to areas zoned exclusively for residential use

d. The zoning of isolated properties for use different from the uses specified by existing zoning laws

23. A defunct shopping center that 10 years ago was built in a commercial-use zone is rezoned for industrial use. This is an example of

a. Spot zoning

b. Nonconforming use

c. Variance

d. Inverse condemnation

24. The value that a taxing authority places on a property refers to the property's

a. Insurance value

b. Loan value

c. Assessed value

d. Appraised value

25. Pursuant to Florida real estate law, which of the following statements is true?

a. In any real estate transaction other than a residential sale, and where the buyer and seller each have assets of $1 million or more, the broker at the request of the customers may designate sales associates to act as single agents for different customers in the same transaction.

b. In any real estate transaction other than a residential sale, and where the buyer and seller have assets of $500,000 or more, the broker at the request of the customers may designate sales associates to act as single agents for different customers in the same transaction.

c. In any real estate transaction, the broker at the request of the customers may designate sales associates to act as single agents for different customers in the same transaction.

d. Dual agency is illegal in Florida, so a broker may not designate sales associates to act as single agents for different customers in the same transaction.

26. The Federal Fair Housing Act does not prohibit

a. Directing people of protected classes away from, or toward, particular areas

b. Religious organizations from limiting the sale, rental or occupancy of dwellings to persons of the same religion

c. Refusal to loan in particular areas

d. Representing that prices will decline, or crime increase, or other negative effects will occur because of the entrance of minorities into particular areas

27. Emily is a single agent for David the seller of a condo, who told Emily that he "really, really" needs to get at least $170,000 for the condo. The day after the listing appears in the MLS, Emily receives two offers: the first offer is all cash for $195,500, and the second offer is for $150,000 with a 60 day loan contingency. Emily should

a. Present the all-cash offer to David and wait to see whether that deal pans out before presenting the second offer

b. Present only the $195,000 offer because the $150,000 offer is considerably below what David has emphatically stated he needs

c. Present both offers to David

d. Present the first offer to David but not the second offer until she sees what other offers come in during the next few days

28. The best use of a property in terms of value is the use most likely to produce the greatest net return (in terms of money or other valued items, such as amenities) over a given period of time is a statement of the principle of

a. Highest and best use

b. Supply and demand

c. Conformity

d. Change

29. David added a pool and an elevator to his two-story house. The resulting value of David's house increased by an amount less than the combined cost of the pool and elevator. This is an example of the principle of

a. Anticipation

b. Contribution

c. Assemblage

d. Progression

30. The Federal Fair Housing Act

a. Limits the applicability of any reasonable local, State or Federal restrictions regarding the maximum number of occupants permitted to occupy a dwelling

b. Prohibits representing that prices will decline, or crime increase, or other negative effects will occur because of the entrance of minorities into particular areas

c. Prohibits discrimination against children with respect to properties occupied solely by persons 62 years of age or older

d. Prohibits conduct against a person because such person has been convicted of the illegal manufacture or distribution of a controlled substance

31. Pursuant to Florida real estate law, which of the following statements is false?

a. A broker's main office may not be in a residential location.

b. The Florida Real Estate Commission (FREC) defines "current mailing address" as the current residential address used by a licensee or permit holder to receive mail through the United States Postal Service.

c. Each active broker must maintain an office, consisting of at least one enclosed room in a building of stationary construction.

d. When the licensee's personal name appears in the advertisement, at the very least the licensee's last name must be used in the manner in which it is registered with the FREC.

32. Primary methods used to estimate reproduction or replacement cost are

a. Square-foot, straight-line, quantity survey

b. Quantity survey, age-life, unit-in-place

c. Unit-in-place, quantity survey, square-foot

d. Square-foot, quantity survey, useful life

33. Loss in value due to changes in utility demand, such as for larger garages, is referred to as

a. Functional obsolescence

b. External obsolescence

c. Economic obsolescence

d. Deferred obsolescence

34. Believing that she is fulfilling her fiduciary duty to her clients, broker Janet encourages them to buy homes in areas with populations primarily of the same nationality as the clients belong to. Broker Janet's actions are

a. Legal because they are in the best interest of their clients

b. Legal because she is, in fact, fulfilling her fiduciary duty to her clients of care and loyalty

c. Illegal because her actions constitute redlining

d. Illegal because her actions constitute steering

35. Alan and Susan's monthly PITI payment is $2,450. Their lender required a PITI ratio of 32%. What is the minimum combined gross monthly income the lender required of Alan and Susan?

a. $7,656.25

b. $7,500

c. $3,602.94

d. None of the above

36. In Florida Administrative Code (FAC), Chapter 61J2-14, "Funds Entrusted to Brokers-Deposits and Escrows," the word "immediately" means

a. The placement of a deposit in an escrow account no later than the end of the third business day following receipt of the item to be deposited

b. The placement of a deposit in an escrow account no later than the end of the second business day following receipt of the item to be deposited

c. The placement of a deposit in an escrow account no later than the end of the next business day following receipt of the item to be deposited

d. None of the above

37. Primary factors for which adjustments in comparable properties must be made in a CMA include all of the following except

a. Square footage

b. Location

c. Financing

d. Mortgage payments on the property

38. Which of the following statements is false?

a. The average price per square foot for a given set of properties is arrived at by adding the per-square-foot cost of each property in the set by the number of properties in the set

b. The median price per square foot of a set of properties is the price per square foot of the property whose price per square foot is such that half of the properties in the set have an equal or lower price per square foot and half have an equal or higher price per square foot

c. Appraisers determine the square footage of a property by using the inside measurement of the property.

d. For a given area, the price per square foot of smaller homes is generally higher than the price per square foot of larger homes

39. Emily is a sales associate who receives on Monday a good-faith deposit from a potential buyer for the purchase of a condo. Emily delivered the good-faith deposit to her broker, Jonathan, the next business day, Tuesday. Assuming no holidays during the week, Jonathan must deposit the good-faith deposit Emily received no later than the end of

a. Tuesday

b. Wednesday

c. Thursday

d. Friday

143

40. Private mortgage insurance (PMI)

a. Is insurance that lenders often require for loans with an LTV more than 75%

b. Must, in general, be canceled when the balance on a conventional loan reaches 78% of the property value and the borrower is current on the loan

c. Insures the borrower

d. Insures the trustee

41. A level payment loan is a loan under which

a. All periodic installment payments are equal, though the amount allocated to principal and interest may vary over the term of the loan

b. Periodic payments consist of interest only

c. The monthly payments pay all of the interest due but not enough of the principal to fully pay off the loan at the end of the loan term

d. Monthly installment payments do not cover all of the interest due

42. During an open house, the listing agent tells a prospective customer: "In my opinion, you won't find a house with a more tranquil, resort-like feel anywhere else in the city." This agent's statement most likely would be considered

a. Negligent misrepresentation

b. Negative fraud

c. Puffing

d. Intentional misrepresentation

43. A Florida broker may place and maintain up to what amount of personal or brokerage funds in a property management escrow account?

a. $250

b. $500

c. $1,000

d. $5,000

44. Nonconforming loans

a. Often sell into the secondary market and usually cost ¼% to ½% less than conforming loans

b. Are loans for homeowners over the age of 62 who have a large amount of equity in their homes

c. Are fully amortized loans

d. Cost borrowers more than loans created in conformance with Federal Housing Finance Agency guidelines

45. Which of the following statements is false?

a. Insurance companies make mortgage loans.

b. The FHA insures mortgage loans.

c. The VA makes mortgage loans.

d. Pension funds make mortgage loans.

46. Carla purchased a home for $200,000 with a 4 % fixed-rate, fully amortized 30-year loan in the principal amount of $170,010. She makes payments of $850 per month. What is the amount of unpaid principal on this loan after the first month's payment?

a. $169,726.70

b. $169,826.67

c. $168,593.30

d. None of the above

47. Each broker must preserve at least one legible copy of all books, accounts, and records pertaining to her or his real estate brokerage business for at least how many years from the date of receipt of any money, fund, deposit, check, or draft entrusted to the broker?

a. 2

b. 3

c. 5

d. 7

48. A clause in a mortgage that states that the lender has the right to accelerate the loan if the secured property is sold or some other interest in the property is transferred

a. An acceleration clause

b. A due-on-sale clause

c. An assumption clause

d. A defeasance clause

49. Under a deed of trust, who typically holds the promissory note?

a. The trustee

b. The beneficiary

c. The trustor

d. The borrower

50. Which of the following is not necessary for a valid escrow?

a. A binding contract between buyer and the seller

b. A market value appraisal

c. An escrow agent

d. Instructions to the escrow agent that impose conditions as to the delivery of instruments and funds on the performance of the stipulated conditions

51. The basic federal antitrust law is the

a. Antitrust Act

b. Free Enterprise and Antitrust Act

c. Sherman Act

d. Unfair Trade Practices Act

52. Amanda is a Florida real estate broker who has received conflicting demands for trust funds from the buyer and seller of an office building. Amanda must institute one of the mandated settlement procedures as set forth in Florida Statutes within how many business days after the last demand?

a. 30

b. 20

c. 15

d. 10

53. Regulation Z implements the

a. Equal Credit Opportunity Act

b. Real Estate Settlement Procedures Act

c. Truth-in-Lending Act

d. Garn-St. Germain Act

54. Emily places her home phone number on the Do-Not-Call Registry. Her phone number will remain on the Registry

a. Until Emily requests that the number be removed or until she discontinues service of that number

b. Only for 1 year, unless renewed

c. Only for 2 years, unless renewed

d. Only for 3 years, unless renewed

55. Which of the following statements is false?

a. As of 2015, a minority of states have adopted the Uniform Electronic Transaction Act.

b. Most states prohibit brokers from running blind ads.

c. An email sent to a client or customer concerning an existing transaction or that updates the client or customer about an ongoing transaction is referred to in the law as a transactional email and is exempt from the CAN-SPAM rules.

d. The Electronic Signatures in Global and National Commerce Act was enacted by Congress to establish the validity of electronic records and signatures regardless of the medium (e.g., email) in which they are created.

56. George is a Florida real estate broker who represented the buyer, Andrew, in the purchase of a home, which purchase was successfully completed. However, Andrew refused to pay the agreed-upon commission that George earned. Which of the following statements is false?

a. George may not place a lis pendens on Andrew's home to secure the payment of his earned commission unless the representation agreement between George and Andrew authorized such action.

b. George may place a lis pendens on Andrew's home to secure the payment of his earned commission regardless as to whether the representation agreement between George and Andrew authorized such action.

c. The Florida Real Estate Commission may suspend or revoke George's license if he places a lis pendens on Andrew's home unless the representation agreement between George and Andrew authorized such action.

d. George may file suit to collect his earned commission.

57. A buyer's agent who is a single agent

a. Owes fiduciary duties to the seller and to the buyer

b. Owes fiduciary duties only to the seller

c. Owes fiduciary duties only to the buyer

d. Owes fiduciary duties to neither the seller nor the buyer

58. Which of the following statements is false?

a. An agency relationship can be created by estoppel.

b. An agency relationship can be created by the equal dignities rule.

c. An agency relationship can be created by ratification.

d. An agency relationship can be created by implication.

59. A property management firm

a. May pay a finder's fee or referral fee to any unlicensed person provided the value of the fee does not exceed $50 per transaction and provided that the referral is for the rental or lease of a unit in the apartment complex.

b. May pay a finder's fee or referral fee to any unlicensed person provided the value of the fee does not exceed $75 per transaction and provided that the referral is for the rental or lease of a unit in the apartment complex.

c. May pay a finder's fee or referral fee to any unlicensed person provided the value of the fee does not exceed $100 per transaction and provided that the referral is for the rental or lease of a unit in the apartment complex.

d. None of the above

60. An agency relationship between an owner of rental properties and a property manager is usually created by a

a. Listing agreement

b. Verbal property management agreement

c. Written property management agreement

d. Designated agent agreement

61. Which of the following statements is false?

a. All states have enacted statutes that require brokers to inform parties to a real estate transaction as to whom the broker is representing.

b. The source of a real estate agent's compensation does not determine agency representation.

c. Some states permit real estate agent associations to set the commission for their members.

d. A dual agent owes fiduciary duties both to the seller and to the buyer.

62. Common law

a. Is law enacted by state legislatures

b. Is law enacted by the federal government

c. Is law developed over time by tradition and law courts

d. Is not one of the sets of laws that govern agency law

63. An agency relationship would not be terminated due to

a. Loss of the agent's license

b. Destruction of the property that is the subject of the agency

c. Death of the president of the principal, which is a corporation

d. The purpose of the agency becoming impossible to fulfill

64. If a broker is a co-owner of a property and the other owners authorize the broker to represent the property for sale,

a. The broker's agency is coupled with an interest

b. The seller may terminate the listing because agency is a personal relationship based on trust and confidence

c. The seller may terminate the agency because of the conflict of interest

d. The broker is what is referred to as a designated agent

65. A residential property was purchased for $375,500. The state documentary transfer fee is $.75 for each $500 or fraction thereof. The property was purchased with $300,500 cash and an assumption of the $75,000 seller's mortgage. Assumed mortgages are exempt from the transfer fee in this state. What was the documentary transfer fee?

a. $562.50

b. $112.50

c. $450.75

d. $450.00

66. The possible fine imposed by the FREC if a Florida real estate licensee misrepresents himself or herself as a Realtor® is

a. $300

b. $500

c. $1,000

d. $5,000

67. Reviewing properties on the Internet, Amanda sees a condo that she is interested in for which broker Bob has the listing. Amanda goes to visit Bob at Bob's office. There, she asks Bob questions about the condo and reviews the comparative market analysis that he prepared for the property. At this point, Bob owes fiduciary duties to

a. Both the seller and Amanda

b. Neither the seller nor Amanda

c. The seller but not Amanda

d. Amanda but not the seller

68. A contingency in a real estate contract

a. Makes the contract unenforceable

b. Makes the contract void

c. Makes one party's obligation to perform dependent on the occurrence of some event

d. Makes the contract valid

69. Joe and John, who are competing brokers, agree to split John's commission 50-50 on the sale of a property John has listed if Joe procures a buyer for the property. This is an example of

a. A legal commission-split agreement

b. Price-fixing

c. Market allocation

d. Tying arrangement

70. Under Florida real estate law, which of the following statements is false?

a. A limited partner of a limited partnership possesses the right and power to bind the partnership.

b. Every partnership registered as a broker must have at least one of its partners licensed or registered as an active broker.

c. Each member of any limited liability company registered as a broker must register as a broker.

d. Each partner of a partnership who expects to deal with the public in the partnership's practice or business as a broker must hold a valid and current active broker's license or registration.

71. Janet sells her condo to Martha for $200,000, closing date May 16. If property taxes on the condo are $1,800 for each six-months, payable in arrears on July 1 and January 1 of each year, and if proration is calculated on the basis of a banker's year (statutory year), what is the proration amount at closing and is who credited/debited?

a. $450 debited to Janet

b. $1,300 debited to Janet

c. $1,350 debited to Janet

d. None of the above

72. Under Florida real estate law, an unlicensed personal assistant of a sales associate may not perform which of the following activities on behalf of the sales associate?

a. Place signs on a property.

b. Negotiate the rent for a condo.

c. Place routine telephone calls on late rent payments.

d. Both b and c.

73. A buyer's agent should recommend that inspections of the buyer's potential new home be conducted by qualified inspectors to do all of the following except

a. Evaluate the home's structure, construction, and mechanical systems

b. Identify all problems that need to be repaired or replaced

c. Estimate the remaining useful life of the plumbing and electrical systems, equipment, structure, and finishes

d. Estimate the value of the property using all appropriate methods of valuation

74. The Florida Division of Real Estate is empowered to investigate an anonymous complaint

a. If the complaint is in writing and is legally sufficient

b. If the alleged violation of law or rules is substantial

c. If the DRE has reason to believe that the violations alleged in the complaint are true

d. All of the above together empower the DRE to investigate an anonymous complaint.

75. A property having a condition that certain persons may find materially negative in a way that does not relate to the property's actual physical condition is called a

a. Natural hazards site

b. Stigmatized property

c. Megan's Law property

d. Materially defective property

76. A licensee should be aware of which of the following when representing buyers or sellers of real property?

a. Underground storage tanks

b. Lead-based paint

c. Asbestos

d. All of the above

77. A Florida real estate broker or sales associate who operates without having a valid and current broker or sales associate license commits

a. A first-degree felony

b. A second-degree felony

c. A third degree felony

d. A misdemeanor

78. If I promise to pay you $20 if you mow my lawn on Tuesday, and you promise to mow my lawn on Tuesday, we have

a. An implied, bilateral contract

b. An express, unilateral contract

c. An implied, unilateral contract

d. An express, bilateral contract

79. A contract that is binding and can be enforced by law is a

a. Void contract

b. Voidable contract

c. Valid contract

d. Written contract

80. The substitution of one contract for another with the intent of extinguishing the original contract is called

a. A novation

b. An assignment

c. An option contract

d. A right of first refusal

81. Joe is a resident manager who receives a 3% commission on rents from an apartment building that he manages. If Joe leases Susan an apartment for three years with rents starting at $750 per month for the first year and increasing by $50 per month for each succeeding year, and if Susan remains in possession of the apartment for the full three years, how much commission will Joe receive from Susan's lease?

a. $864

b. $810

c. $216

d. None of the above

82. A Florida sales associate has recently had numerous judgments against him arising out of multiple real estate transactions. The maximum amount that the claimants involved in these numerous judgments may receive from the Florida Real Estate Recovery Fund is

a. $150,000 in aggregate

b. $50,000 to each of the claimants

c. $150,000 to each of the claimants

d. $500,000 in aggregate

83. Liquidated damages refer to

a. A court order that requires a person to perform according to the terms of a contract.

b. Water related destruction or diminution in the value of property.

c. A sum of money that the parties agree, usually at the formation of a contract, will serve as the exact amount of damages that will be paid upon a breach of the contract.

d. An amount equal to 3% of the good-faith deposit.

84. In Florida, property taxes are due and payable on

a. January 1 of each year or as soon thereafter as the certified tax roll is received by the tax collector

b. March 1 of each year or as soon thereafter as the certified tax roll is received by the tax collector

c. April 1 of each year or as soon thereafter as the certified tax roll is received by the tax collector

d. November 1 of each year or as soon thereafter as the certified tax roll is received by the tax collector

85. A listing agreement in which the seller agrees to list the property with only one broker who will receive the agreed-on commission if, during the term of the listing, the property sells or if the broker procures a buyer who is ready, willing, and able to meet all of the terms of a sale contained in a listing agreement, regardless of who is responsible for procuring the buyer is called

a. An exclusive agency listing

b. A net listing

c. An option listing

d. An exclusive right to sell listing

86. In a percentage lease, the percentage of the gross receipts of the tenant's business that is added to lease payments is

a. Usually equal to the percent markup used in the tenant's business

b. Usually greater than the percent markup used in the tenant's business

c. Usually independent of the percent markup used in the tenant's business

d. Usually dependent on the percent markup used in the tenant's business

87. When a tenant vacates the premises at the termination of the lease, if the landlord does not intend to impose a claim on the tenant's security deposit, the landlord must, within how many days, return the security deposit together with any accrued interest, if applicable?

a. 45

b. 30

c. 15

d. 10

88. After Olivia received an offer of $375,000 for her house from Bob, she counteroffered at $395,000. Before Bob accepted the counteroffer, Olivia received an offer from John for $399,000. Olivia can accept John's offer if

a. She notifies Bob of the better offer and gives him a chance to match John's offer

b. John's offer satisfies every term of her offer to Bob

c. She withdraws her counteroffer to Bob before his acceptance is delivered to her

d. She waits to hear from Bob

89. If the optionee of an option contract does not complete the purchase within the specified option period

a. The optionee typically will forfeit the option fee

b. The optionor typically must refund the option fee

c. The optionee may renew the option by paying the same option fee again

d. The optionor may force the optionee to complete the purchase by bringing an action for specific performance

90. A lease of a single-family home is

a. A contract and a conveyance

b. A contract but not a conveyance

c. A conveyance but not a contract

d. Neither a contract nor a conveyance

91. In Florida, a month-to-month tenancy may be terminated by either party

a. By giving not less than 30 days' notice prior to the end of any monthly period

b. By giving not less than 15 days' notice prior to the end of any monthly period

c. By giving not less than 10 days' notice prior to the end of any monthly period

d. By giving not less than 7 days' notice prior to the end of any monthly period

92. Pursuant to the Florida Vacation Plan and Timesharing Act, a purchaser of a timeshare has an unwaivable right to cancel the purchase contract until how many days after signing the contract or after delivery of all required documents, whichever is later?

a. 7 business days

b. 7 calendar days

c. 10 business days

d. 10 calendar days

93. An example of a chattel real is a

a. Contract to purchase a single-family home

b. Contract to purchase a refrigerator

c. a One-year lease of a condo

d. a Court order that authorizes the sheriff to remove a tenant from leased premises

94. Amelia purchases a condominium unit from the developer. Amelia may cancel the purchase contract up to how many days after signing the purchase agreement with the developer?

a. 10 calendar days

b. 10 business days

c. 15 calendar days

d. 15 business days

95. A quitclaim deed contains

a. No warranties

b. A covenant of seisin

c. A covenant of quiet enjoyment

d. A covenant against encumbrances

96. Which, if any, of the following statements is (are) true?

a. A Florida real estate licensee may not render an opinion that the title to any property sold is good or merchantable, except when correctly based upon a current opinion of a licensed attorney at law

b. A Florida real estate licensee *must* advise a prospective purchaser to consult her or his attorney on the merchantability of the title or to obtain title insurance.

c. Both a and b.

d. Neither a nor b.

97. Which, if any, of the following statements is (are) true?

a. Florida real estate licensees must give the principal(s) a legible, signed, true and correct copy of the listing agreement within 48 hours of obtaining the written listing agreement.

b. A written listing agreement may contain an automatic renewal clause.

c. Both a and b.

d. Neither a nor b.

98. A cloud on title is

a. A chronological summary of all grants, liens, wills, judicial proceedings, and other records that affect the property's title

b. A complete chronological history of all documents affecting the title to a property

c. An examination of all relevant public documents to determine whether there exist any potential defects against the title

d. Any document, claim, lien, or other encumbrance that may impair the title to real property or cast doubt on the validity of the title

99. Florida imposes transfer taxes associated with the transfer of real property, including which of the following?

a. Documentary stamp tax on deeds and other instruments relating to real property or interests in real property.

b. Documentary stamp tax on promissory or nonnegotiable notes, written obligations to pay money, or assignments of wages or other compensation.

c. Intangible tax on new mortgages.

d. All of the above.

100. Martin purchased a Florida single-family home for $295,400, paying $59,080 cash, assuming the seller's outstanding mortgage of $95,000, and the taking out a new mortgage in the amount of $141,220. The documentary stamp tax on the notes resulting from this transaction would be

a. $827.05

b. $332.50

c. $494.55

d. None of the above

ANSWERS TO PRACTICE EXAM #4:

Abbreviations used in this Practice Exam are:

DBPR — Department of Business and Professional Regulation
FAC — Florida Administrative Code
FREC — Florida Real Estate Commission
FS — Florida Statutes

1. **a.** An applicant for a sales associate or broker license must possess and submit a Social Security number to allow screening of applicants and licensees by a child support agency to assure compliance with child support obligations, but an applicant need not be a U.S. citizen or a Florida resident.

2. **c.** As a general rule, the distinguishing feature between real property and personal property is that real property is fixed and immovable, where as personal property is movable.

3. **a.** FS, 475.180(2)(a), states that any "resident licensee who becomes a nonresident shall, within 60 days, notify the commission of the change in residency and comply with nonresident requirements.

4. **d.** A section of a township contains 640 acres.
Therefore, ¼ × ¼ × ¼ × 640 acres = 10 acres.

5. **b.** FS, 177.031(18), states that "'subdivision' means the division of land into three or more lots, parcels, tracts, tiers, blocks, sites, units, or any other division of land; and includes establishment of new streets and alleys, additions, and resubdivisions; and, when appropriate to the context, relates to the process of subdividing or to the lands or area subdivided."

6. **d.** A lien that is a created by law is an involuntary lien. Involuntary liens can be specific (e.g., a mechanics lien) or general (e.g., a judgment lien).

7. **a.** Special assessments are specific and involuntary liens.

8. **a.** Most subdivisions use the lot, block and tract system (also referred to as the recorded map or recorded plat system) to give a legal description of the land.

9. **c.** FS, 475.183(2)(b), provides that any "license that has been involuntarily inactive for more than 2 years shall automatically expire. Once a license expires, it becomes null and void without any further action by the commission or department. Ninety days prior to expiration of the license, the department shall give notice to the licensee."

10. **d.** An easement is terminated if the person who benefits from the easement acquires the servient tenement.

11. **d.** An encroachment is a thing affixed under, on, or above the land of another without permission. Examples of encroachments include overhanging tree branches and buildings, roofs, or fences that cross a boundary line.

12. **b.** FS, 475.23, provides that a "license shall cease to be in force whenever a broker changes her or his business address, a real estate school operating under a permit issued pursuant to s. 475.451 changes its business address, or a sales associate working for a broker or an instructor working for a real estate school changes employer. The licensee shall notify the commission of the change no later than 10 days after the change, on a form provided by the commission."

13. **a.** To exercise eminent domain, an appropriate governmental body must satisfy certain requirements, including that the owner must be paid a just compensation.

14. **a.** Examples of the use of police power in regard to real property include the creation and enforcement of zoning codes, building codes, subdivision regulations, and property setbacks. Deed restrictions are examples of private restrictions.

15. **c.** The Comprehensive Environmental Response, Compensation, and Liability Act (also referred to as the Superfund Law) is intended to clean up sites contaminated with pollutants and toxic wastes.

16. **c.** FS, 475.278(2), states that a "transaction broker provides a limited form of representation to a buyer, a seller, or both in a real estate transaction but does not represent either in a fiduciary capacity or as a single agent."

17. **d.** In zoning, a strip of land to separate, or to ease the transition from, one use to another is referred to as a buffer zone.

18. **c.** Conditions (often called conditions subsequent) that are placed in a deed can have serious consequences if breached; namely, forfeiture of title.

19. **b.** $95,000 × .07 = $6,650 (vacancy and uncollectible rents losses).
$95,000 - $6,650 = $88,350 (effective gross income).
$88,350 - $21,000 (operating expenses) = $67,350 (NOI). *Note that monthly mortgage payments are disregarded when calculating net operating income.*
$67,350 ÷ .095 = $708,947 (rounded).

20. **d.** FS, 475.272(1), disallows dual agency in the state of Florida.

21. **a.** The Civil Rights Act of 1866 was the first law that protected persons against racial discrimination in the lease or purchase of real property.

22. **a.** Inclusionary zoning refers to city and county zoning ordinances that require builders to set aside a given portion of new construction for people of low to moderate incomes.

23. **a.** Spot zoning refers to the zoning of isolated properties for use different from the uses specified by existing zoning laws.

24. **c.** Assessed value is the value a taxing authority places on the property, which may differ significantly from the property's market value.

25. **a.** FS, 275.2755(1), provides that in any real estate transaction other than a residential sale, and where the buyer and seller each have assets of $1 million or more, the broker at the request of the customers may designate sales associates to act as single agents for different customers in the same transaction.

26. **b.** The FFHA does not prohibit religious organizations from limiting the sale, rental or occupancy of dwellings to persons of the same religion.

27. **c.** FS, 475.278(3)(a)8, states that single agents must present "all offers and counteroffers in a timely manner, unless a party has previously directed the licensee otherwise in writing." As stated in the question, David did not direct Emily in writing not to present him with offers less than $170,000; therefore, Emily must present both offers to David in a timely manner.

28. **a.** The principle of highest and best use states that the best use of a property in terms of value is the use most likely to produce the greatest net return (in terms of money or other valued items, such as amenities) over a given period of time.

29.   b. The principle of contribution (also referred to as the principle of diminishing marginal returns) states that improvements made to a property will contribute to its value or that, conversely, the lack of a needed improvement will detract from the value of the property.

30.   b. The Federal Fair Housing Act prohibits representing that prices will decline, or crime increase, or other negative effects will occur because of the entrance of minorities into particular areas.

31.   a. Florida Administrative Code (FAC), 61J2-10.022, provides that a broker's main office "may be in a residential location, if not contrary to local zoning ordinances, provided the minimum office requirements are met and the required broker's sign is properly displayed." Choice b is correct pursuant to FAC, 61J2-10.038. Choice c is correct pursuant to FS, 475.22(1). Choice d is correct pursuant to FAC, 61J2-10.025(2).

32.   c. Primary methods used to estimate reproduction or replacement cost include the square-foot method, the quantity survey method, and the unit-in-place method.

33.   a. Loss in value due to changes in utility demand, such as for larger garages, is referred to as functional obsolescence.

34.   d. National origin is a protected class under the Federal Fair Housing Act, and the practice of directing people of protected classes away from, or toward, particular areas is an illegal practice known as steering.

35.   a. $2,450 ÷ (grossly month income) = .32.
Therefore, grossly monthly income = $2,450 ÷ .32 = $7,656.25.

36.   a. FAC, 61J2-14.008(3) provides as follows: "'Immediately' means the placement of a deposit in an escrow account no later than the end of the third business day following receipt of the item to be deposited. Saturdays, Sundays and legal holidays shall not be considered as business days."

37.   d. Primary factors for which adjustments in comparable properties must be made in a CMA include square footage, location, and financing.

38.   c. Appraisers determine the square footage of a property by using the *outside* measurement of the property.

39.   c. FAC, 61J2-14.010, states that every broker receives from a sales associate a good-faith deposit must "immediately" deposit the good-faith deposit. FAC, 61J2-14.008(3), provides that the word "immediately" means "the placement of a deposit in an escrow account no later than the end of the third business day following receipt of the item to be deposited." FAC, 61J2-14.009, provides that receipt "by a sales associate or any other representative of the brokerage firm constitutes receipt by the broker." *Therefore, even though Jonathan did not have the good-faith deposit in hand until Tuesday, he nevertheless was in "receipt" of the good-faith deposit on Monday, pursuant to FAC, 61J2-14.009.*

40.   b. The Homeowner's Protection Act requires that PMI be canceled when the mortgage balance reaches 78% of the property value (77% for "high risk loans") and the borrower is current on the loan.

41.   a. A level payment loan is a loan under which all periodic installment payments are equal, though the amount allocated to principal and interest may vary over the term of the loan.

42.   c. Couched as an opinion and absent an intent to deceive, this statement would most likely be viewed as puffing — mere sales talk.

43.   **d.** FAC, 61J2-14.010(2), provides as follows: "A broker may place and maintain up to $1,000 of personal or brokerage funds per each *sales* escrow account. A broker may place and maintain up to $5,000 of personal or brokerage funds per each *property management* escrow account." (emphasis added)

44.   **d.** Nonconforming loans cost borrowers more than loans created in conformance with Federal Housing Finance Agency guidelines.

45.   **c.** The VA does not make mortgage loans; it guarantees certain mortgage loans.

46.   **a.** $170,010 × .04 ÷ 12 = $566.70 (first month's interest)
$850 - $566.70 = $283.30 (first month's principal payment)
$170,010 - $283.30 = $169,726.70 (principal balance after first month's payment).

47.   **c.** FS, 475.5015, provides that each "broker shall preserve at least one legible copy of all books, accounts, and records pertaining to her or his real estate brokerage business for at least 5 years from the date of receipt of any money, fund, deposit, check, or draft entrusted to the broker."

48.   **b.** A due-on-sale clause states that the lender has the right to accelerate the loan — declare the entire outstanding principal and interest due and payable immediately — if the secured property is sold or some other interest in the property is transferred.

49.   **b.** Under a deed of trust, the lender (beneficiary) holds the promissory note; the trustee holds legal title with power to sell upon default by the borrower.

50.   **b.** A market value appraisal is not a necessary element of a valid escrow.

51.   **c.** The basic *federal* antitrust law is the Sherman Act passed in 1890. The other answers are names of antitrust laws of various states.

52.   **a.** FAC, 61J2-10.032(1)(a), provides that a "real estate broker, upon receiving conflicting demands for any trust funds being maintained in the broker's escrow account, must provide written notification to the Commission within 15 business days of the last party's demand and the broker must institute one of the settlement procedures as set forth in Section 475.25(1)(d)1., Florida Statutes, within 30 business days after the last demand."

53.   **c.** The set of regulations that implemented TILA is known as Regulation Z.

54.   **a.** Once a phone number is on the registry, it will remain there until the person requests that the number be removed or until the person discontinues service of that number.

55.   **a.** As of 2015, 47 states have adopted UETA. Illinois, New York, and Washington have not adopted UETA but have their own laws recognizing electronic signatures.

56.   **b.** FS, 475.42(i), states that a real estate licensee may not place a lis pendens or other encumbrance upon the real property of a client or customer who fails to pay a commission, unless otherwise agreed in writing by the client or customer. FAC 61J2-24.00(3)dd), provides that a violation of FS, 475.42(i) can result in an administrative fine of $250 to $2,500 and suspension or revocation of license.

57.   **c.** A buyer's agent who is a single agent owes fiduciary duties only to the buyer.

58.   **b.** An agency relationship can be created by estoppel, ratification, and application, but not by the equal dignities rule.

59.   **d.** FS, 475.001(13), provides that a property management firm or an owner of an apartment complex may pay a finder's fee or referral fee to an unlicensed person *who is a tenant in such apartment complex* provided the value of the fee does not exceed $50 per transaction and provided that the referral is for the rental or lease of a unit in the apartment complex. FS, 475.001(13), further provides that it is a violation for a property management firm or an owner of apartment complex to pay a finder's fee to an unlicensed person who is not a tenant of the apartment complex.

60.   **c.** An agency relationship between an owner of rental properties and a property manager is usually created by a written property management agreement.

61.   **c.** Pursuant to federal antitrust law, all real estate compensation is subject to negotiation in every state.

62.   **c.** Common law is law developed over time by tradition and law courts, and is often referred to as case law.

63.   **c.** Because a corporation is considered a separate entity, the death of corporate officers of either the principal or the agent would not terminate the agency.

64.   **a.** If a broker is a co-owner of a property and the other owners authorize the broker to represent the property for sale, the broker's agency is coupled with an interest.

65.   **c.** $300,500 = $500 × 601$.
$601 × \$.75 = \$450.75$.

66.   **a.** FAC 61J2-10.027, states that no "licensee shall use an identification or designation of any association or organization having to do with real estate unless entitled to use such identification or designation." FAC 61J2-24.002(2)(v), provides that the use of the name or identification of an association or organization when the licensee is not in good standing or otherwise not entitled to use same is $300.00.

67.   **c.** Amanda would not become Bob's client until they sign an agency representation agreement. Amanda must, however, be treated honestly, fairly, and in good faith by Bob.

68.   **c.** A real estate purchase contract usually contains several contingencies, which make one party's obligation to perform dependent on the occurrence of some event, such as obtaining adequate financing.

69.   **a.** A broker's agreement with a cooperating broker to split the commission in a particular real estate transaction is permissible under antitrust laws.

70.   **a.** FS, 620.1302, provides that a "limited partner does not have the right or the power as a limited partner to act for or bind the limited partnership."

71.   **c.** Using the banker's year of 30 days per month, at the closing Janet is in arrears in her payment of taxes by 15 days in May and $4 × 30 = 120$ days for January through April, total 135 days. Because there are 180 days in six months of a banker's year, the per day tax rate on the $1,800 tax bill is $10. Therefore, 135 days $× \$10$ per day $= \$1,350$, which should be debited to Janet and credited to the Martha.

72.   **b.** FS, 475.01(1)(a), presents a list of activities brokers and sales associates may perform that require real estate licenses. One of those activities is the negotiating of rents. Choices a and c are activities that unlicensed personal assistants may perform pursuant to the guideline "Permissible Activities of an Unlicensed Assistant" approved by the FREC, which, at the time of this writing, can be found at www.myfloridalicense.com/dbpr/re/documents/Permissibleactivitiesrev092009.pdf.

73.   **d.** Estimating the value of a property is the job of an appraiser, not a home inspector.

74.   **d.** FS, 475.021(1), provides that all "services concerning this chapter, including, but not limited to, recordkeeping services, examination services, legal services, and *investigative services, and those services in chapter 455* necessary to perform the duties of this chapter shall be provided by the Division of Real Estate." (emphasis added) Additionally, FS,

455.225(1)(a), provides that the "department may investigate an *anonymous complaint* if the complaint is in writing and is legally sufficient, if the alleged violation of law or rules is substantial, and if the department has reason to believe, after preliminary inquiry, that the violations alleged in the complaint are true." (emphasis added)

75. **b.** A stigmatized property is a property having a condition that certain persons may find materially negative in a way that does not relate to the property's actual physical condition.

76. **d.** A licensee should be aware of any property issue that is a material fact.

77. **c.** FS 475.42(1)(a), provides that a "person may not operate as a broker or sales associate without being the holder of a valid and current active license therefor. Any person who violates this paragraph commits a felony of the third degree."

78. **d.** The contract between us is express (verbal) and bilateral (each of us has made a promise to the other).

79. **c.** A valid contract is a contract that is binding and can be enforced by law. Not all written contracts are valid.

80. **a.** A novation is the substitution of one party for another (in which case the first party is entirely excused from performing under the contract) or the substitution of one contract for another with the intent of extinguishing the original contract.

81. **a.** 750×12 months = $9,000. 800×12 months = $9,600. 850×12 months = $10,200. Total for the three years his $28,800. $28,800 \times 3\%$ = $864 commission.

82. **a.** FS, 475.484(4), provides that payments from the Real Estate Recovery Fund "for claims based upon judgments against any one broker or sales associate may not exceed, in the aggregate, $150,000."

83. **c.** Liquidated damages are a sum of money that the parties agree, usually at the formation of a contract, will serve as the exact amount of damages that will be paid upon a breach of the contract.

84. **d.** FS, 197.133, provides that all "taxes shall be due and payable on November 1 of each year or as soon thereafter as the certified tax roll is received by the tax collector."

85. **d.** An exclusive right to sell listing is a listing agreement in which the seller agrees to list the property with only one broker who will receive the agreed-on commission if, during the term of the listing, the property sells or if the broker procures a buyer who is ready, willing, and able to meet all of the terms of a sale contained in a listing agreement, regardless of who is responsible for procuring the buyer.

86. **d.** The percentage of gross charged is usually dependent on the percent markup used in the tenant's business.

87. **c.** FS, 83.49(3)(a), provides that upon "the vacating of the premises for termination of the lease, if the landlord does not intend to impose a claim on the security deposit, the landlord shall have 15 days to return the security deposit together with interest if otherwise required, or the landlord shall have 30 days to give the tenant written notice by certified mail to the tenant's last known mailing address of his or her intention to impose a claim on the deposit and the reason for imposing the claim."

88. **c.** Until Olivia receives an acceptance of her counteroffer from Bob, she is free to accept another offer regardless of whether it is superior to Bob's offer.

89. **a.** In an option contract, the optionor grants the optionee the right to purchase property for a specific sum at any time during the option term without creating an obligation by the optionee to do so. For this option right, the optionee pays the optionor a specified option fee, which is typically not refundable if the option is not exercised.

90. **a.** A lease transfers an estate in the real property leased. A lease also constitutes an executory bilateral contract between landlord and tenant that governs such matters as the landlord's maintenance of the property and the tenant's duty to make lease payments.

91. **b.** FS, 83.57(3), provides that a month-to-month tenancy may be terminated by either party "by giving not less than 15 days' notice prior to the end of any monthly period."

92. **d.** FS, 721.07(2)(d)(1.) requires that a purchaser of a timeshare has an unwaivable right to cancel the purchase contract until 10 calendar days after signing the contract or after delivery of all required documents, whichever is later.

93. **c.** A lease constitutes an executory bilateral contract between landlord and tenant that governs such matters as the landlord's maintenance of the property and the tenant's duty to make lease payments. This contract aspect of a lease creates privity of contract between landlord and tenant, which makes a leasehold estate a chattel real — an interest in land that is less than a freehold estate and is also a form of personal property governed by laws applicable to personal property.

94. **c.** FS 719.503(1)(a) (1.), states that anyone who purchases a condominium unit from the developer may cancel the purchase contract by delivering notice of the purchaser's intention to cancel within 15 calendar days of the execution of the contract by the buyer.

95. **a.** A quitclaim deed contains no warranties of any kind.

96. **c.** FS 475.25(1)(j), provides that the FREC may discipline any licensee who has "rendered an opinion that the title to any property sold is good or merchantable, except when correctly based upon a current opinion of a licensed attorney at law, or has failed to advise a prospective purchaser to consult her or his attorney on the merchantability of the title or to obtain title insurance."

97. **d.** FS, 475.25(1)(r), provides that a licensee must "give the principal(s) a legible, signed, true and correct copy of the listing agreement within 24 hours of obtaining the written listing agreement. The written listing agreement shall contain no provision requiring the person signing the listing to notify the broker of the intention to cancel the listing after such definite expiration date." The last sentence implies that a written listing agreement may not contain an automatic renewal clause.

98. **d.** Any document, claim, lien, or other encumbrance that may impair the title to real property or cast doubt on the validity of the title is a cloud on title.

99. **d.** Choice a is provided for by FS, 201.02. Choice b is provided for by FS, 201.08. Choice c is provided for by FS, 199.133.

100. **d.** FS, 201.08, provides for a documentary stamp tax on promissory notes in the amount of $.35 per $100 or fraction thereof. This applies to both notes for new mortgages as well as on notes for assumed mortgages. Martin's assumed and new mortgages total $236,320. $236,320 \div $100 = $2,363.20. Therefore, because the documentary stamp tax on promissory notes is $.35 per $100 *or fraction thereof*, the documentary stamp tax on the promissory notes related to this transaction is 2,364 × $.35 = $827.40.

Made in the USA
Lexington, KY
11 August 2016